A Beginner's Guide to Economic Research and Presentation

A Beginner's Guide to Economic Research and Presentation

Jeffrey A. Edwards

A Beginner's Guide to Economic Research and Presentation
Copyright © Business Expert Press, 2013.
All rights reserved. No part of this publication may be reproduced, stored in a retrieval system, or transmitted in any form or by any means—electronic, mechanical, photocopy, recording, or any other except for brief quotations, not to exceed 400 words, without the prior permission of the publisher.

First published in 2013 by
Business Expert Press, LLC
222 East 46th Street, New York, NY 10017
www.businessexpertpress.com

ISBN-13: 978-1-60649-832-3 (paperback)
ISBN-13: 978-1-60649-833-0 (e-book)

Business Expert Press The Economics Collection

Collection ISSN: 2163-761X (print)
Collection ISSN: 2163-7628 (electronic)

Cover and interior design by Exeter Premedia Services Private Ltd. Chennai, India

First edition: 2013

10 9 8 7 6 5 4 3 2 1

Printed in the United States of America.

Abstract

Conducting good research is critical to any student today. Writing good research papers is equally important—yet many students have not been given the proper tools to convey cogently the results of their research. *A Beginner's Guide to Economic Research and Presentation* is intended to address and redress this need.

This book is literally a step-by-step approach to the writing of an undergraduate or graduate level research paper in the field of economics. The primary audience for this book consists of those students who have not conducted research or written a research paper, or those students that are looking for ways of improving their research skills. Most books concerned with research writing are broadly applied. They approach the subject generally, which is to say that they don't lay out a *particular* path to conducting research. Yet a specific path offering a specific focus to writing research is exactly what is needed for most students. This book provides that focus. For example, *A Beginner's Guide to Economic Research and Presentation* doesn't cover a dozen different search engines to perform a literature review; it specifies only EconLit. Nor is the student left to decide what scholarly publications are important ones to review; the book emphasizes only the use of journal impact factors found through RePEc to rank journal articles and their importance to the literature at large. Whereas other books provide an overview of how to present research, with only cursory suggestions and tips, *A Beginners Guide to Economic Research and Presentation* provides precise details on all aspects of research writing, including how many PowerPoint slides one should prepare for presentations and how much content should be on each slide. In short, unlike other books, this book provides a *specific* approach to conducting research, writing a paper, and presenting its material.

Keywords

regression, regression models, inference, equation editing, table design, research topics, research questions, research hypotheses, literature reviews, data collection, formatting, drafting, presentation

This book is dedicated to my wife Catherine.

Contents

Introduction xi

Chapter 1   Basic Regression Analysis and Inference 1

Chapter 2   More Sophisticated Regression Analysis
and Inference 13

Chapter 3   Basic Equation Editing and Table Design 31

Chapter 4   Choosing a Research Topic, Question,
and Hypothesis 39

Chapter 5   Literature Reviews 45

Chapter 6   Data Collection and Formatting 53

Chapter 7   Drafting and Refining the Paper 61

Chapter 8   Pointers on Presenting to a Live Audience 71

Conclusion 77
Notes 79
Index 81

Introduction

This book is an introduction to writing a research paper in the field of economics. The primary audience for this book consists of students who have either not conducted research and/or written a research paper, or only broached the activity in a cursory manner. Such an audience might include undergraduate business majors in general, economics majors in particular, or graduate students studying in fields related to economics. And while this last group will probably find the first chapter on econometrics too rudimentary, the remainder of the book will be of great value even to that population of individuals.

For the instructor, the book is organized in a way that I have found yields the most understandability among the students when faced with performing research and writing a paper for the first time; but it is not written in the way other similar books are. Specifically, most books in this area are written as broadly applied guides to writing research papers. By broadly applied I mean that they don't lay out a *particular* path to conducting research. This is a problem simply because it is exactly that path that is needed for most students; this book provides that focus.

As mentioned in the abstract, this book doesn't cover a plethora of search engines to perform a literature review; it specifies only the primary search engine in economics, EconLit. It doesn't leave it to the student to decide what scholarly publications are important ones to review; it emphasizes only the use of journal impact factors found through RePEc to rank journal articles and their importance to the literature at large. This book doesn't just provide an overview of how to present research with some cursory suggestions and tips; it provides precise details on how many PowerPoint slides one should have and exactly how much content should be on those slides. In other words, unlike other books, this book provides a *specific* approach to conducting research, writing a paper, and presenting its material.

Another way this book differs from the others is that it focuses on the empirical tools of research before addressing the topic of forming research questions and hypotheses. I've often wondered when teaching my own courses out of other books, exactly how can a student choose an effective research question if they do not yet know *how* to model that question? More importantly, how can a student decide on a question if they do not know what statistical inference is? I have found that students who have learned or refreshed themselves with basic modeling and statistical inference early in class choose more sophisticated questions and hypotheses on which to perform their research, conduct better literature reviews regarding that research, and tend to write better papers overall. This, in my opinion, is simply because the rest of the semester is grounded *within* the context of empirical inference, which is the tool with which they will ultimately conduct their work. Books that focus on empirical work late in the curriculum force the student to design their research agenda before they know how to actually apply that agenda, effectively putting the cart before the horse.

Since I have taught many undergraduate and graduate courses specifically related to performing research in economics, the organization of this book reflects my own views on how to obtain the best results possible for relatively novice writers, and therefore the best papers possible from your students. I am certainly not indicating that your students will be able to write grade A papers after reading this book, but I do believe that at the least there will be a statistically significant improvement in their performance relative to what their performance would have been had they not read it.

General Outline

The book starts with the basics of econometric modeling. The first chapter is dedicated to linear modeling, programming in Stata and Excel, and inference from linear models. At this point, I leave any additional concepts such as heteroskedasticity, dependency, logarithmic transformation, etc., to the instructor to teach. Having said that, one knows that a research paper at this level does not necessarily need to address these issues to be a well-written, first-time research paper in economics. And even though I use Stata and mention it as the preferred econometric software package, I probably don't cover enough programming in Stata to satisfy the more rigorous instructors. However, I purposely leave the door open for these instructors to include a more comprehensive programming portion in their class curriculum. This is simply because the book is so short and basic. It really should only take half to two-thirds of the semester to instruct out of this book, leaving sufficient time to add material such as programming and other misspecification issues like dependency, heteroskedasticity, etc., and still finish the curriculum before the semester's end.

Starting at such a basic level of econometrics may be redundant to some in higher performing undergraduate and graduate programs; I truly don't expect instructors in Harvard's economics department to teach out of this portion of the book. This is because these students would likely have already taken a couple of courses on econometrics proper, rendering at least the first chapter obsolete. But, it is probably the case at most schools that the curriculum sequencing we desire to implement for majors (i.e., passing an econometrics course prior to a seminar course) does not always work out that way. Nevertheless, this book moves on in the second chapter to a way of modeling and drawing inference that may not be taught in an econometrics course the way I teach it.

I focus heavily on the separation between what I term "statistical" omitted variable bias and "theoretical" omitted variable bias. Within the context of this book, statistical omitted variable bias results from leaving out a squared right-hand-side variable when one is needed. We know that if a linear model is used when the relationship is quadratic, biased inference will result. In this section, I also focus on calculating maximums and minimums, and how these apply within relevant sample spaces. I place emphasis on this area simply because the vast majority of theoretical relationships in economics are non linear in nature mostly due to some sort of diminishing returns. On the other hand, theoretical omitted variable bias exists when some variable, z, is left out of the conditioning set altogether. This type of bias results purely as a function of a theoretical relationship that influences the correlation between the variable of interest and the dependent variable. I have found that students understand these concepts better when separated in this fashion. From here I take the reader into basic fixed-effects modeling using panel data, and even touch on within transformations.

The remainder of the book structure focuses on performing literature reviews, how to read research papers, drafting, redrafting, finalizing the text, and presentation. Having published dozens of articles myself, I mostly rely on what works well for just me. Yet, I also realize that the research I perform is many levels of sophistication higher than the research these students will perform. To that end, I focus on "tricks of the trade" that will help the student bypass the rather technical aspects of writing a paper for publication in a top research journal, yet produce enough information to earn a good grade in a research seminar course.

In the end, I believe this book outperforms the others on the market simply because it is so simple. The instructor will be able to expand on this material without sacrificing precious class time, and the student will be able to use this book as a practical guide to writing a successful term paper. One would hope that performing good basic research in this field will expand the marketability of the student when they graduate, and this book should go a long way in attaining that objective. With that in mind, I hope you enjoy it!

CHAPTER 1
Basic Regression Analysis and Inference

This book's approach to regression analysis is truly basic. We won't go into issues such as the sum of squared errors, heteroskedasticity, statistical hypothesis testing (as opposed to economic hypothesis testing), t-statistics, f-statistics, etc. While all of these issues are very important for more sophisticated circles, it's simply not necessary to perform economic research at its most basic level. I will, however, use both Microsoft Excel as well as the regression package Stata. Even though we will be performing basic econometrics that can all be executed with Excel, the reader is encouraged to use Stata as this software is very easy to use with the student version of Stata costing well under $100. Once learned, Stata can become one of the most useful tools for performing any kind of empirical research after the student graduates college.

What Is a Regression Model?

We start with what a regression is meant to do—it is to generate an averaging line within a set of observations that are simultaneously determined by two variables. As with all lines, this line will have a slope and an intercept. Most of us remember grade school and the formula

$$y = mx + b \tag{1.1}$$

whereby, y is one variable, x another variable, and m and b are the line's slope and intercept, respectively; we use very similar notations in regression analysis. We use something called a regression model that takes the form

$$y = a_0 + a_1 x + e \tag{1.2}$$

where y is usually called the dependent or left-hand-side variable, x the independent or right-hand-side variable, a_0 the line's intercept, and a_1 is the line's slope; in regression jargon a_0 and a_1 are known as the estimators or coefficients. The new term in (1.2) which is not in (1.1) is e. This is what makes a regression different from a mere line. This is because a regression generates an estimate of the relationship between x and y, and the estimate itself is the averaging line. With any estimate there is a certain amount of error, and this is what e represents. So in essence we have an estimated line

$$y = \hat{a}_0 + \hat{a}_1 x \tag{1.3}$$

with e being the difference between the actual relationship and the estimated relationship reflected in (1.3). The coefficients $\hat{a}_0$ and $\hat{a}_1$ are the estimates of the relationship's intercept and slope, respectively.

Estimation and Inference

To make this clearer, assume we have two made-up variables, whereby x = yearly income of 10 home owners and y = each individual's respective cost of their homes—all in dollars. Table 1.1 lists these values and Figure 1.1 plots them on a graph. As expected, there is a positive correlation between annual income and the price of the houses these individuals purchased, that is, we expect that as incomes increase, people will purchase more expensive homes. Figure 1.2 shows the same plot as Figure 1.1, but with an averaging line through the dots on the graph.

Table 1.1.

y = House price ($)	x = Annual income ($)
427,900	147,000
78,500	54,600
66,950	47,325
247,900	92,500
110,500	67,450
85,000	51,230
399,000	111,250
410,900	119,500
156,500	72,400
105,900	60,750

To estimate the slope and intercept using *Excel*, one would

1. Open up an Excel spreadsheet and in the first cell of the first column and first row, enter a title for the income data (let's use *income* as the title for simplicity), and in the first cell of the second column, enter a title for the house price data (let's use *price* as the title).
2. In the subsequent cells underneath each title enter the data as shown in the table.
3. Click on the Data tab at the top and then click on Data Analysis; a pop-up box will appear. Scroll to Regression and click on it. Another pop-up box will appear.
4. With the cursor in the Input Y Range box, highlight the house price column including the title of the column. Move the cursor to the

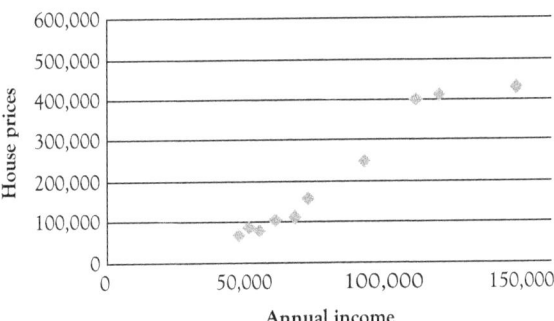

Figure 1.1. Scatter plot of income on house prices.

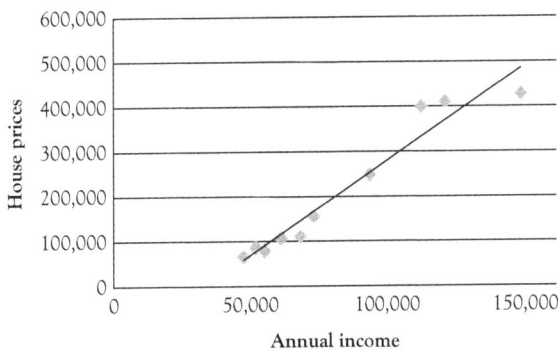

Figure 1.2. Estimated relationship between income and house prices.

Input X Range box, and highlight the income column including the title. Also, click the Labels box to the left of the Y and X input range boxes. We do this to tell Excel that the first cell contains letters, not numbers.
5. Click the OK button.

In *Stata*, one would complete the following steps in Stata's Do-file:

A. Perform steps 1 and 2 from the Excel instructions. Open Stata and click on the Data Editor (Edit) icon—it's the spreadsheet icon with a pencil in it. In your Excel spreadsheet, highlight your entire data set including titles and copy it. Then in your Stata Data Editor, click on Edit, click on Paste, and click on Treat First Row as Variable Names. Close the data editor.
B. Back in the Stata screen, click on Window, then on Do-file Editor and New Do-File; a blank pop-up window will appear.
C. Type in the following command: reg price income
D. In the top bar of the Do-file Editor, click on the Execute (do) icon.

If you performed the Excel task, you will see

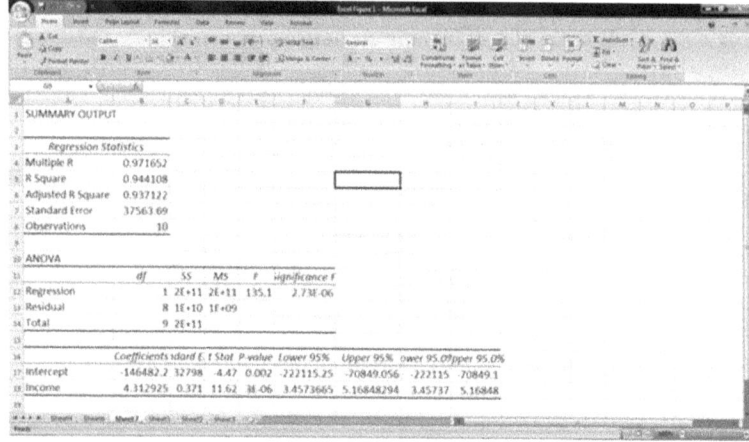

Figure 1.3. Excel regression output for income.

And with Stata, you will see

```
. reg price income

      Source |       SS       df       MS              Number of obs =      10
-------------+------------------------------           F(  1,     8) =  135.13
       Model |  1.9068e+11     1  1.9068e+11           Prob > F      =  0.0000
    Residual |  1.1288e+10     8  1.4110e+09           R-squared     =  0.9441
-------------+------------------------------           Adj R-squared =  0.9371
       Total |  2.0197e+11     9  2.2441e+10           Root MSE      =   37564

------------------------------------------------------------------------------
       price |      Coef.   Std. Err.      t    P>|t|     [95% Conf. Interval]
-------------+----------------------------------------------------------------
      income |   4.312925   .3710133    11.62   0.000     3.457366    5.168483
       _cons |  -146482.2   32798.34    -4.47   0.002    -222115.2   -70849.06
------------------------------------------------------------------------------
```

Figure 1.4. Stata regression output for income.

The reader can quickly see why Stata is the preferred package for regression analysis: it's simply easier to use and formats the output in a more readable way. Hence, from this point forward, we will only show Stata output, but will provide instructions to perform each operation in Excel as well. For now let us just focus on the numbers in the bottom two rows of figures 1.3 and 1.4; we'll get to what some of the other numbers mean later.

As we can see, the estimate of the intercept, _cons in Stata, is −$146,482.20, and the estimate for the slope is 4.312. Superficially one would conclude from this result that if incomes were zero, the average home price would be −$146,482.20, and for every $1000 dollar increase in income level one would add $4312 to the price of a home. However, there aren't any home prices that are negative, at least to my knowledge. If one believes that house prices are at a minimum bounded below by zero, then one would have to resort to basic mathematics to complete this interpretation. Using the notation above, we can write this output in the form of a linear equation as $Price = -\$146,482.20 + 4.312\, Income$. We can set price equal to zero and solve for income to get $Income = \$33,924$; in other words, on an average, individuals with incomes that are less than or equal to $33,924 per year will not own a home (or more precisely, own a home worth zero dollars).

Far more important is the interpretation of something known as a *marginal effect*. This concept is the focal point of nearly all economic research. Simply put, a marginal effect refers to a one-unit change in one variable causing some amount of change in another variable (this amount could be zero, or no change which we will address later in the book). Unfortunately, this is where we have to use a little basic calculus to determine the marginal effect.

Whenever someone hears the word *margin* used in the context of economics, one should always think derivative (not financial derivative, but mathematical derivative). Readers of this book may be aware of basic economic concepts, such as marginal revenue, marginal cost, marginal product, etc. These are actually the derivatives of the revenue, total cost, and total product functions, respectively. Mathematically, one would represent a derivative of y with respect to x as $\frac{\partial y}{\partial x}$. (For those who are more mathematically inclined, I use partial derivative notation here simply to let instructors who want to go into interaction effects do so without having to change notation in their lecture(s).) To take a derivative of a function $y = ax^r$, we would perform the operation $\frac{\partial y}{\partial x} = rax^{r-1}$. In our case, we have the function $y = a_0 + a_1 x + e$; so performing the same operation on this equation would yield the derivative $\frac{\partial y}{\partial x} = a_1 x^{1-1}$. But since any variable to the power 1−1 equals 1, then we have $\frac{\partial y}{\partial x} = a_1 * 1$, or simply $\frac{\partial y}{\partial x} = a_1$. Therefore, the slope of the regression line is the marginal effect! In other words, the marginal effect of a $1,000 increase (decrease) in annual income, on an average, will increase (decrease) the purchase price of someone's home by $4,312. However, our inference is not yet complete.

Statistical inference requires two things, and sometimes three. At a minimum, inference requires an interpretation of the sign of the coefficient estimates (i.e., are they positive or negative), and analysis of the *statistical significance* of the estimates, especially the slope coefficients. The third component of inference, one which is not always addressed in research, is the magnitude of the coefficient estimate. Many times the estimate itself is less important than the sign of the estimate—an issue we will approach later in this section.

With regard to statistical significance, it may seem like the number 4.312 is a substantial distance from zero, but if there is a lot of variation in the data, we may not be *confident* that it is zero. To determine whether an estimate is significantly different from zero we will use something called p-values.

Interpreting a p-value takes some imagination. The data in Table 1.1 is a sample; it is not the entire population of income earners and respective home owners. And nearly all data one collects has this property. So assume the population consists of 100 home owners/income earners and we pull a sample of 10 observations from that population. We run the regression we just ran, and get estimates of the coefficients equal to what we just got. Now, put those observations back into the population, and randomly draw another 10 observations. Run a new regression. The estimates you get from this regression may be similar but not the same because most likely the sample observations you drew this time were not identical to those drawn earlier. Then replace these observations back into the population. Draw a new sample and run another regression. The same thing will occur—you will get a new estimate of the slope and intercept that will likely be different from the first two sets of estimates for the same reason. If you do it 1,000 times, say, you will get a distribution of estimates of the slope and intercept. This distribution should resemble a bell-shaped curve with the center of the bell being concentrated around the value of the coefficient had one used the population instead of a bunch of samples (see Figure 1.5). Furthermore, as with any continuous variable, these values may span the entire real number line. The values of the estimated slope we obtained in the previous paragraphs could very well have been negative. Therefore, statistical significance must be calculated as a two-sided determination within a probability distribution.

To be 90% confident that the value you obtained is significantly different from zero results from determining whether 95% of the draws out of the 1,000 total draws, does not cross zero in value. We can only be 90% confident, and not 95%, because theoretically the estimate can take on any value on the real number line; if the distribution was on the negative side of zero then the upper tail of the distribution would come into consideration as well. View Figure 1.5 and imagine that if we were to draw a sample 1,000 times, would we get a positive (negative) value of our slope coefficient at least 950 times? If so, then I can be at least 90% confident that that estimate is in fact not zero. This would equate to a *p*-value of no more than 0.100. The *p*-value would equal 0.100 because if the probability of the coefficient taking on any value is 100%, and we have a 5% cutoff in each tail of the distribution, then 100% − 5% − 5% = 90%; 90% is the minimum amount of confidence we would have that the estimate is not zero. Since the *p*-value tells us the amount of the distribution that lies in the tails, and in this case no more than 10% of the estimates would, the *p*-value would be no more than 0.100.

As another example, assume that we again make 1,000 draws, but we only get a positive value of the slope coefficient 925 times, meaning that 75 estimates were negative. If the distribution was mostly on the negative side of zero, the upper tail would also hold 75 positive values. In either case, zero would lie *inside* the respective bounds of the 90% confidence interval in Figure 1.5. Since 75 is 7.5% of 1,000, then we could only be 100% − 7.5% − 7.5% = 85% confident that the estimate is not zero. In this case the *p*-value would equal 0.150, or 15% written in percentage rather than decimals.

Hence, the lower the *p*-value, the more confident I can be that the coefficient estimate is not in fact zero. We call this a *statistically significant coefficient* or a *statistically significant relationship*. Our cutoff for the remainder of the book will be 90% confidence, or a *p*-value of 0.100 or less.

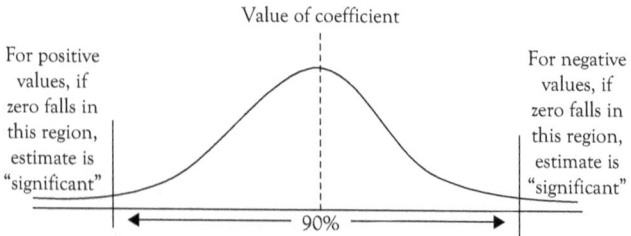

Figure 1.5. Coefficient distribution.

From the values in Figure 1.4, we see that the slope coefficient estimate has a *p*-value of 0.000, and the intercept has a *p*-value of 0.002. This means that we can be 100% and 99.8% confident, respectively, that these values are not zero. We would consider these estimates to be statistically significant. If, for instance, the slope coefficient was not significant indicated by a *p*-value greater than 0.100, then we could not make the statement that incomes influence purchase price. In fact, we would then conclude that incomes "have no statistically significant effect on the purchase price of a home."

In its totality, the full inference we would draw from this regression is that as incomes rise, so does the purchase price of the home that income earners buy. Furthermore, for every $1,000 increase in incomes, purchase price rises by $4,132. But one must ask whether this result would be the same if we controlled for other variables that influence someone's purchase of a home, such as the number of children in a family? We can certainly assume that the more children in a family, the bigger house one needs and the more likely someone is to purchase a larger, and probably more expensive home. What if we held the number of children constant, would the marginal effect of income on house price be as large? We should add a variable to the regression that reflects the number of children for each individual in our sample and find out.

Table 1.2 is the same as Table 1.1, but with an additional column that lists the number of children for each individual sampled; for instance, a sampled person who makes $92,500 per year with three kids purchased

Table 1.2.

y = House price ($)	x = Annual income ($)	z = Number of children
427,900	147,000	3
78,500	54,600	0
66,950	47,325	1
247,900	92,500	3
110,500	67,450	1
85,000	51,230	0
399,000	111,250	4
410,900	119,500	5
156,500	72,400	1
105,900	60,750	0

a house valued at $247,900. We still have a linear regression model, but now it looks like $y = a_0 + a_1 x + a_2 z + e$, whereby z is the number of children in the household. Running a regression like we did before but now highlighting both the income and children column for the x input range in Excel, or for Stata, adding children to the command in line (c), we get the following output

```
. reg price income children

      Source |       SS       df       MS              Number of obs =      10
-------------+------------------------------           F(  2,     7) =  166.20
       Model |  1.9780e+11     2   9.8901e+10          Prob > F      =  0.0000
    Residual |  4.1654e+09     7    595052278          R-squared     =  0.9794
-------------+------------------------------           Adj R-squared =  0.9735
       Total |  2.0197e+11     9   2.2441e+10          Root MSE      =   24394

-------------------------------------------------------------------------------
       price |      Coef.   Std. Err.      t    P>|t|     [95% Conf. Interval]
-------------+-----------------------------------------------------------------
      income |   3.000613   .4493558     6.68   0.000     1.938055    4.06317
    children |   28931.66   8362.251     3.46   0.011     9158.081    48705.24
       _cons |  -90423.97   26761.55    -3.38   0.012    -153705    -27142.95
-------------------------------------------------------------------------------
```

Figure 1.6. *Regression output for income and number of children.*

Drawing inference from these results we find that, as expected, holding the number of children constant substantially changes the marginal effect of income on the price someone will pay for a home. Now for every $1,000 increase in income, house price increases by only $3,000, not $4,132—this result is also a statistically significant result like the previous one. We can draw inference from the estimate of the coefficient for the children variable as well. It is significant with a p-value of 0.011, and can be interpreted as: on an average, each additional child in the household increases the purchase price of a house by $28,931, with holding income constant.

However, we cannot determine how expensive a home someone making $100,000 per year would purchase without placing an actual value to the number of children. This is because the interpretation of the intercept is not the same as it was when there was only one variable on the right-hand side. While the previous results could be graphed in two dimensions, as shown in Figure 1.2, and therefore we could simply look at the graph and guess what price this individual would pay for their home, in this case we would have to graph this relationship in three dimensions. Here, the intercept is actually a common intercept for both relationships between income and price, and children and price. To interpret this outcome like we did before, we would have to say something like "an individual making $100,000 per year in income, with 2 children, would purchase a house equal to $-90,423 + 3.000*100,000 + 28,931*2 = \$267,439$. The same individual with no children would purchase a home priced at $-90,423 + 3.000*100,000 + 28,931*0 = \$209,584$. And imagine how problematic this interpretation would become if there were more than two right-hand-side variables. These interpretation issues are precisely why many researchers stop inference at statistical significance and sign of the marginal effect and do not comment on the calculation of the estimated dependent variable.

At this point, I have said all I can about drawing inference on the estimated marginal effect. There is one other statistic that some consider important. Out of all the numbers in Tables 1.4 and 1.6, truly the only other bit of information that may be needed for basic research in economics would be the adjusted R-squared value. The R-squared is formally known as a sample correlation coefficient and tells the researcher how well their entire model fits the data. Specifically, it is a ratio of the variation in y that is explained by the entire set of right-hand-side variables, to the total variation in y. The model that generated the output for Figure 1.4 explains 93% of the variation in house prices, while the addition of the children variable adds roughly another 4% to that number.

We use the adjusted R-squared value instead of the nonadjusted value because we want to discount the R-squared by the number of right-hand-side variables we have in our model. Since no coefficient value is actually zero, even if it has a very large p-value, adding additional x's to our model would increase its explanatory power of y. Therefore we need to adjust for this and the adjusted R-squared does exactly that.

I mentioned earlier that reflecting on the R-square value "may" be important information for a researcher. But to be honest, most good researchers ignore it. The reason is simple. Is a model with an R-squared value of 0.90 any better than one with an R-squared value of 0.30? Only in one instance—when forecasting a time series process. Model fit is critical when one wants to predict what inflation will be in the United States next quarter; but it is meaningless in the vast majority of economic research where the marginal effect is what is important. Especially for a cross-country growth researcher such as myself, low R-squared values are a common outcome; but, it doesn't mean that my model is a "bad" model. It simply means that there are many factors outside of my variable set that explain the dependent variable—variables I probably don't have access to, or are simply not relevant to the research question I am asking.

Suggested Readings

For an introduction to other aspects of econometrics, one should read

Naghshpour, S. (2012). *Regression for economics*. New York, NY: Business Expert Press.

Gujarati, D. N. (2003). *Basic econometrics*. New York, NY: McGraw-Hill Publishing.

For a more comprehensive introduction to Stata programming, one should read

Baum, C. F. (2006). *An introduction to modern econometrics using Stata*. College Station, TX: Stata Press.

Baum, C. F. (2009). *An introduction to Stata programming*. College Station, TX: Stata Press.

CHAPTER 2

More Sophisticated Regression Analysis and Inference

So far we have covered very basic regression analysis of a linear function and drawn inference from the results. Now we carry regression analysis into the realm of quadratic modeling, omitted variable bias, and within transformations using actual data from the World Bank's World Development Indicators Database. But first, we will have to discuss some basic database constructs and equation formatting.

Types of Data and Equation Formatting

There are three basic types of data used in economic research—time series data, cross-sectional data, and panel data. A basic time series model with one left-hand-side variable and one right-hand-side variable can be written as

$$y_t = a_0 + a_1 x_t + e_t. \tag{2.1}$$

The reader will notice that the only difference between this form and the form depicted in Chapter 1 is the subscript, t. This subscript denotes a time series regression using time series data. Time series data is data that consists of observations of one individual over time. This is in contrast to a cross-sectional model written as

$$y_i = a_0 + a_1 x_i + e_i. \tag{2.2}$$

In this form, the t subscript is replaced with an i subscript. Hence, a cross-sectional regression uses cross-sectional data that is at one point in time (or an average of longitudinal observations) across individuals, i. This is exactly the type of data we used for the house price example in Chapter 1.

Panel data combines the two dimensions with a typical model being written as

$$y_{it} = a_{i0} + a_1 x_{it} + e_{it}. \qquad (2.3)$$

A panel regression, then, is performed using a data set that crosses multiple individuals, i, over time, t. Even though this is probably the most common type of data used in economic research, it is also the most complicated data to work with at a sophisticated research level. What makes it complicated is the time dynamic component. However, at our level of sophistication our only concern will be the a_{i0}'s in (2.3) and how to deal with them. This means that we will ignore the time dimension and time series analysis altogether, and focus only on the cross-sectional analysis of panel data.

Quadratic Modeling and Inference

What is a quadratic model? Basically, it's any model that has a marginal effect of the form

$$\frac{\partial y}{\partial x} = a_1 + 2a_2 x. \qquad (2.4)$$

In order to obtain this particular marginal effect, model (2.3) for instance would have to take the form

$$y_{it} = a_0 + a_1 x_{it} + a_2 x_{it}^2 + e_{it}. \qquad (2.5)$$

In other words, a quadratic regression model allows for the possibility that the relationship between x and y is a nonlinear one—specifically either concave up or concave down. A good example in economics of a concave down relationship is a production function, and a concave up relationship is an average total cost function. Since it is so common in economics to assume diminishing returns in output to pretty much every type of input, at least in the short run, quadratic relationships make theoretical sense in many economic applications. But there is also a statistical concern why quadratic relationships should always be tested for in regression analysis.

If a researcher wants to investigate the "true," or more appropriately, the "more accurate" relationship between x and y, a nonlinear averaging line may be better than a straight line. Figure 2.1 depicts an arbitrary scatter plot where a linear function is estimated for data that is nonlinear.

It is clear that assuming this relationship is a linear one is inappropriate. The actual values at the ends of the plot are below the line, while those in the middle are all above the line. A more appropriate depiction would be that in Figure 2.2. The reader can see that if he/she needed to estimate a future value of y given some value of x, the line in Figure 2.2 would give a more accurate estimate than in Figure 2.1.

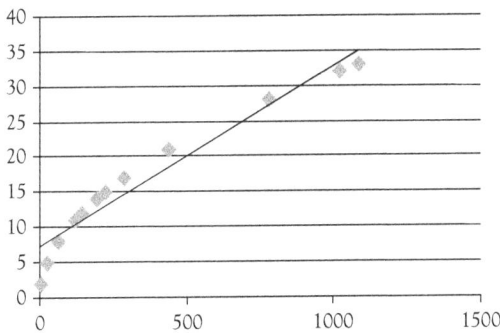

Figure 2.1. Example plot of linear function.

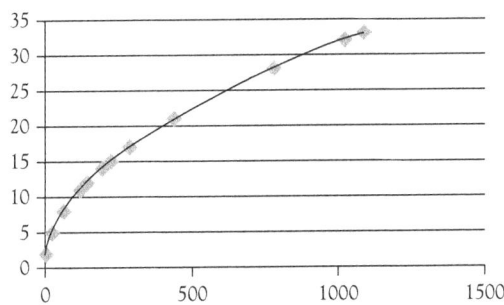

Figure 2.2. Example plot of nonlinear function.

Actually estimating (2.5) is easy. But first, we must load our Excel sheet with data and perform the linear regression as we did in Chapter 1. We need to perform this regression first as a reference in order to see exactly how our inference changes, if any, when we include the squared health variable.

Appendix 2.1 contains the core data that we will use for the remainder of this chapter. The data consists of four variables spanning eight countries and the years 2005–2009 for each country, resulting in 40 total observations. The variables are growth in per capita GDP in U.S. dollars based in the year 2000 (Growth), healthcare spending by the public sector as a percentage of GDP (Health), gross domestic investment as a percentage of GDP (Inv), and the population growth rate in percentages (Pop). The variable Growth will be our left-hand-side variable, and Health, Inv, and Pop our right-hand-side variables. The variable Health will be our variable of interest. Therefore, *we will be testing to what extent healthcare spending by the public sector affects economic growth in a country.* All data come from the 2011 version of the World Development Indicators database, constructed by the World Bank. To load the data, perform steps 1 and 2 from Chapter 1 using the data in Appendix 2.1. If you are using Stata, also perform step A from Chapter 1.

Go ahead and execute the simple linear regression but this time using Growth as your left-hand-side variable instead of house prices, and Health as your right-hand-side variable instead of income levels. The output should look like

```
. reg growth health

      Source |       SS       df       MS              Number of obs =      40
-------------+------------------------------           F(  1,    38) =   15.16
       Model |  93.8421675     1  93.8421675           Prob > F      =  0.0004
    Residual |  235.280669    38  6.19159655           R-squared     =  0.2851
-------------+------------------------------           Adj R-squared =  0.2663
       Total |  329.122836    39  8.43904709           Root MSE      =  2.4883

------------------------------------------------------------------------------
      growth |      Coef.   Std. Err.      t    P>|t|     [95% Conf. Interval]
-------------+----------------------------------------------------------------
      health |  -.5546634   .1424727    -3.89   0.000    -.8430843   -.2662424
       _cons |   4.079862   .7663237     5.32   0.000     2.528521    5.631204
------------------------------------------------------------------------------
```

Figure 2.3. Simple linear regression.

The output of the simple linear regression tells us that there exists a statistically significant negative correlation between public sector healthcare spending and growth. The inference we can draw from this output is that a one percentage point increase in public spending will translate into a 0.554 percentage point decrease in economic growth. The question remains whether this inference is accurate or not. To answer this we must proceed to test whether this relationship is a nonlinear one.

Our initial quadratic equation will take the form

$$Growth_{it} = a_0 + a_1 Health_{it} + a_2 Health_{it}^2 + e_i, \qquad (2.6)$$

and our marginal effect of interest will be

$$\frac{\partial Growth}{\partial Health} = a_1 + 2a_2 Health_{it}. \qquad (2.7)$$

To construct a squared health spending variable in Excel, first insert a blank column next to the Health column. Then highlight the first cell in that column and title that column Health_sq. Let us assume that Column A contains the year, B the country's name, C the Growth observations, D the Health observations, and therefore the highlighted cell will be contained in Column E. Highlight the cell directly below the cell containing the title, then type into the function bar (it has the symbol f_x next to it)

=D2*D2

and hit enter on your keyboard. Then place the cursor over the bottom right corner of that cell until a plus sign appears and drag to the bottom of the data set. This will automatically drag the command to the last observation of the last country. You should now have squared values of Health in Column E. Alternatively, in Stata's Do-file write the following:

gen health_sq=health^2

and run the Do-file as you did in D of Chapter 1.

Once the squared healthcare variable has been constructed, in Excel perform steps 3–5 from Chapter 1 just like you did for the regression you just ran, but now highlighting all cells in both Health and Health_sq for the *x*-input range, and highlight the Growth column for the *y*-input range. In Stata, write the following command in the next line of the Do-file:

reg growth health health_sq

but before you run the Do-file, place a * in front of the command you wrote to generate the squared healthcare variable; in other words, that command should now look like

*gen health_sq=health^2

The purpose of the * is to tell Stata that the squared variable has already been generated. If you don't do this, you will get an error returned as Stata will recognize that the variable already exists (for curiosity's sake, try running the Do-file without making this adjustment).

Run the Do-file as before. The output screen should look like

```
. reg growth health health_sq

     Source |       SS       df       MS              Number of obs =      40
------------+------------------------------           F(  2,    37) =   12.67
      Model |  133.781054     2  66.8905268           Prob > F      =  0.0001
   Residual |  195.341783    37  5.27950764           R-squared     =  0.4065
------------+------------------------------           Adj R-squared =  0.3744
      Total |  329.122836    39  8.43904709           Root MSE      =  2.2977

------------------------------------------------------------------------------
      growth |      Coef.   Std. Err.      t    P>|t|     [95% Conf. Interval]
-------------+----------------------------------------------------------------
      health |   1.686608   .8254309     2.04   0.048     .014126    3.35909
   health_sq |  -.2706326   .0983963    -2.75   0.009    -.4700024   -.0712627
       _cons |   1.564342   1.156382     1.35   0.184    -.77871    3.907394
------------------------------------------------------------------------------
```

Figure 2.4. Quadratic regression.

The inference we would draw from this set of output would be as follows. First, the coefficient for the squared healthcare variable is significant with a *p*-value of 0.009. The estimated marginal effect would be

MORE SOPHISTICATED REGRESSION ANALYSIS AND INFERENCE   19

$$\frac{\partial Growth}{\partial Health} = 1.686 - 2 * 0.270\, Health_{it}, \quad (2.7)$$

or alternatively

$$\frac{\partial Growth}{\partial Health} = 1.686 - 0.540\, Health_{it}. \quad (2.8)$$

Since the second derivative equals -0.540, we know this function would be concave downward and therefore have a maximum. Hence, increases in public healthcare spending as a percentage of GDP would increase growth up to the maximum, and decrease growth thereafter. But where is the maximum and does it lie within the given sample range of healthcare spending values? To calculate the maximum we would solve for $Health_{it}$ as follows

$$1.686 - 0.540\, Health_{it} = 0 \quad (2.9)$$

$$-0.540\, Health_{it} = -1.686 \quad (2.10)$$

$$Health_{it} = -1.686 / -0.540 \quad (2.11)$$

$$Health_{it} = 3.122. \quad (2.12)$$

Therefore, the maximum of this estimated function lies at a public healthcare spending level of 3.122% of GDP. Examining the data set, the Health variable ranges from 0.699% to 8.349%, meaning that the maximum of the relationship lies inside the sample range, and therefore comes into play when drawing inference. Hence, over the relevant sample range increasing public sector healthcare spending as a percentage of GDP would increase growth at a decreasing rate up to approximately 3.122% in spending, but decrease growth at an increasing rate thereafter. And if our sample of countries were a random selection (which it isn't for the purpose of our experiment here in this chapter), we would conclude that on average countries with public sector health spending up to 3.122%, a further marginal increase in spending would increase growth. On the other hand, countries with spending levels above this will actually increase their growth rates by reducing current spending, not increasing it further. In our sample, Bangladesh, Pakistan, and Kenya, would each benefit in terms of increased growth by increasing their public healthcare spending, while Columbia, the Netherlands, Italy, the United States, and the United Kingdom, would all benefit by reducing spending. If we were to assume this relationship were linear and stop there, the conclusions we would draw, that is, increasing spending lowers growth for *all* countries, would have been a biased conclusion.

While nonlinearity in the relationship of interest was of obvious concern, since assuming a linear relationship when the true relationship is nonlinear would be an incorrect assumption, two other concerns regularly rear their heads in economic research—theoretical omitted variable bias and model calibration. Let us address the latter concern first.

Model Calibration and Theoretical Omitted Variable Bias

When modeling data, there are certain empirical regularities that one should expect to find; and if one doesn't, there is probably something wrong with the model and/or data that was used. To test whether there is something wrong, a researcher will always include in their regression a variable for which theory dictates should have a particular relationship with the left-hand-side variable, and for which the vast majority of empirical studies supports this theoretical relationship. This variable we call a calibration variable.

Out of the remaining variables in our data set, Pop and Inv, Inv would be the better calibration variable. This is because we know with near certainty that it should have a strong positive relationship with growth. Harking back to basic macroeconomics and the expenditure approach to calculating GDP, investment enters additively on the right-hand side. Furthermore, the two most popular variables used in production function analysis are labor and capital. Investment is often used as a proxy for capital since investment is a flow variable like growth, and capital is a stock variable. To this end, we will re-run our regression adding Inv to equation (3); the output we obtain will be

```
. reg growth health health_sq inv

  Source |       SS       df       MS              Number of obs =      40
---------+------------------------------            F(  3,    36) =   10.32
   Model |  152.161692     3  50.7205641            Prob > F      =  0.0000
Residual |  176.961144    36  4.91558733            R-squared     =  0.4623
---------+------------------------------            Adj R-squared =  0.4175
   Total |  329.122836    39  8.43904709            Root MSE      =  2.2171

-----------------------------------------------------------------------------
  growth |     Coef.   Std. Err.      t    P>|t|    [95% Conf. Interval]
---------+-------------------------------------------------------------------
  health |   1.367529   .8133872    1.68   0.101    -.2820966    3.017155
health_sq|  -.2154205   .0991448   -2.17   0.036    -.4164955   -.0143456
     inv |   .338183    .1748876    1.93   0.061    -.0165056    .6928716
   _cons |  -5.283042   3.712692   -1.42   0.163    -12.81273    2.246646
-----------------------------------------------------------------------------
```

Figure 2.5. Model calibration regression.

We find that investment does indeed have a statistically significant and positive relationship with growth as expected, meaning that we can have fairly high confidence that our dataset and model are adequately constructed.

Our final concern is theoretical omitted variable bias. Most researchers simply call it omitted variable bias, but I like to differentiate it from an objective and purely statistical bias. A perfect example of statistical omitted variable bias is the inclusion of the squared public health spending variable. Had we not included that permutation of healthcare spending, our original inference would have been biased. And while we could hypothesize why there would exist a nonlinear relationship between growth and healthcare spending, for the most part, testing for it was simply to paint a more statistically accurate picture of the relationship with growth. Theoretical omitted variable bias is different. The idea of it only relies on theory. We may have such bias if (a) there exists a variable that we have access to that is correlated with growth, and (b) it is simultaneously correlated with our variable of interest—in this case, public healthcare spending. The Pop variable satisfies the two criteria for theoretical omitted variable bias.

First, it is correlated with growth as it enters into a production function as a proxy for labor; and when included with investment, determines a Malthusian relationship between population growth and growth in per capita GDP.[1] In this theory, an increase in a country's population level, holding investment constant, would likely strain food resources to the point that it drags down growth rates. Therefore, we can conclude that population growth should be negatively correlated with growth. Secondly, Pop should also be correlated with public sector healthcare spending. It makes sense that countries with high population growth should divert more resources toward keeping that population healthy. And if we assume that (a) the government is elected by the people, or (b) the government is run by a dictatorship (two extreme cases), then we would expect the government in particular to spend more on healthcare to increase the probability that it gets reelected, or reducing the probability that it gets overthrown. To this end, population growth should be positively correlated with public sector healthcare spending.

One of the empirical aspects of theoretical omitted variable bias is that, unlike the calibration variable, it does not need to have a statistically significant relationship with the LHS variable (especially when controlling for other variables), nor must its coefficient take on a particular sign. This is because there may exist discerning theoretical arguments in either direction whereby opposite relationships would cancel themselves out (resulting in statistical insignificance). The reason it is included is simply to subtract out properties and information contained in it that may influence the relationship of interest—in this case, the relationship between growth and healthcare spending.

Adding the population variable to the equation, we get the output

```
. reg growth health health_sq inv pop

      Source |       SS       df       MS              Number of obs =      40
-------------+------------------------------           F(  4,    35) =    9.34
       Model |  169.884683     4  42.4711707           Prob > F      =  0.0000
    Residual |  159.238154    35  4.54966154           R-squared     =  0.5162
-------------+------------------------------           Adj R-squared =  0.4609
       Total |  329.122836    39  8.43904709           Root MSE      =   2.133

      growth |      Coef.   Std. Err.      t    P>|t|     [95% Conf. Interval]
-------------+----------------------------------------------------------------
      health |   1.530883   .7868915     1.95   0.060    -.0665917    3.128358
   health_sq |  -.3111707   .1070116    -2.91   0.006    -.5284159   -.0939255
         inv |   .0702889   .2161762     0.33   0.747    -.3685722     .50915
         pop |  -2.214614   1.122068    -1.97   0.056    -4.492533    .0633047
       _cons |     4.9249    6.28551     0.78   0.439    -7.835364    17.68516
```

Figure 2.6. *Omitted variable bias regression.*

We notice from this output that population growth does have a statistically significant and negative relationship with growth in real per capita GDP. Furthermore, we find that the coefficient for domestic investment becomes insignificant. This doesn't matter because the Malthusian effect outlined earlier inherently ties investment with population growth. Having said that, we find that there was substantial theoretical omitted variable bias in the output of Figure 2.4. Performing the same calculations that we did in equations (7)–(10), the maximum with the inclusion of investment is at a healthcare spending level of 3.179%, but the inclusion of population growth reduced this amount by nearly 23% to 2.459%. Given that our original calculation in (10) was 3.122%, it wasn't substantially influenced by the inclusion of investment and therefore investment wasn't an omitted variable in the theoretical sense. But we can indeed conclude that population growth rates do influence the relationship between growth and public sector healthcare spending and therefore was an omitted variable.

Our modeling is nearly complete. The inference we can draw at this point is that countries with levels of public healthcare spending below 2.459% of GDP will increase growth with an increase in spending, but at a decreasing rate. Countries above that amount, however, should reduce spending if they want to enhance growth. But there is one last specification issue that must be addressed as we are using panel data to model our relationship of interest. This issue has to do with the fact that until now we have assumed that the constant term is the same for all countries. In other words, that the conditional mean growth rate for each country is the same. Given our particular set of sample countries, this seems a very unlikely assumption to make. Now we must correct for it.

Fixed Effects Regression

Until now we have been ignoring the i in the a_{i0} from equation (iii). In order to account for it, we must generate a constant term for each country. Using our relatively small data set with only eight countries, this is easy. For data sets with a far larger i-dimension, we would have to use a little basic algebra. That said, let's do the easy one first.

If the i-dimension of your data set is small, constructing what are called dummy variables are the easiest way of letting each i have its own constant term. A dummy variable is simply a binary, zero-one variable that takes the value 1 for each observation pertaining to each country, and 0 otherwise. The rule of thumb is to construct one fewer dummy variables than you have countries, letting the original constant term represent the country left out. This means that the coefficient estimate for each country is the *difference* between that country's intercept coefficient, and the intercept coefficient of the country that was left out of the construction of the dummy variables. As an example, let us assume we only have two countries, then our model (2.13) would take the form

$$Growth_{it} = a_{01} + a_{02}D_2 + a_1 Health_{it} + a_2 Health_{it}^2 + e_i, \quad (2.13)$$

where D_2 takes the value 1 for the country two observations, and zero otherwise. Therefore, when $D_2 = 1$, the value of the intercept coefficient estimate for country two is $a_{01} + a_{02}$; when $D_2 = 0$, which it does for the country one observations, we get the estimate for the country one intercept which will be simply a_{01}. Hence, the estimate of a_{02} is the difference between the estimate for country one's intercept and country two's intercept.

Proceeding with constructing the dummy variables for seven of the eight countries in our sample, in Excel we would simply label the first cell of seven blank columns by typing in D1 through D7; in subsequent cells we would enter a 1 whenever that cell pertains to a particular country, and 0 for all other cells in that column. The partial screen shot in Figure 2.7 shows

	Country	Growth	Inv	Pop	Health	Health_Sq	D1	D2	D3	D4	D5	D6	D7
2	Colombia	3.142	19.659	1.532	5.289	27.973521	1	0	0	0	0	0	0
3	Colombia	5.07	21.333	1.511	5.199	27.029601	1	0	0	0	0	0	0
4	Colombia	5.327	22.091	1.487	5.105	26.061025	1	0	0	0	0	0	0
5	Colombia	1.241	20.861	1.461	4.928	24.285184	1	0	0	0	0	0	0
6	Colombia	-0.6	20.541	1.429	5.405	29.214025	1	0	0	0	0	0	0
7	Banglades	4.298	24.527	1.577	1.12	1.2544	0	1	0	0	0	0	0
8	Banglades	5.024	24.651	1.517	1.24	1.5376	0	1	0	0	0	0	0
9	Banglades	4.883	24.464	1.462	1.189	1.413721	0	1	0	0	0	0	0
10	Banglades	4.699	24.208	1.415	1.044	1.089936	0	1	0	0	0	0	0
11	Banglades	4.294	24.372	1.378	1.064	1.132096	0	1	0	0	0	0	0
12	Italy	-0.086	20.733	0.739	6.465	41.796225	0	0	1	0	0	0	0
13	Italy	1.457	21.094	0.569	6.563	43.072969	0	0	1	0	0	0	0
14	Italy	0.741	21.208	0.733	6.311	39.828721	0	0	1	0	0	0	0
15	Italy	-2.072	20.721	0.767	6.643	44.129449	0	0	1	0	0	0	0
16	Italy	-5.652	18.912	0.648	7.35	54.0225	0	0	1	0	0	0	0
17	Kenya	3.167	18.699	2.621	1.732	2.999824	0	0	0	1	0	0	0
18	Kenya	3.558	19.082	2.631	1.702	2.896804	0	0	0	1	0	0	0
19	Kenya	4.221	19.417	2.638	1.612	2.598544	0	0	0	1	0	0	0
20	Kenya	-1.094	19.717	2.642	1.537	2.362369	0	0	0	1	0	0	0
21	Kenya	-0.08	20.09	2.639	1.466	2.149156	0	0	0	1	0	0	0

Figure 2.7. Dummy variable construction.

what the top half of the resulting matrix would look like. (I couldn't show the whole matrix because my screen isn't big enough, but you'll get the idea.)

We then run our regression as we did previously, but now highlighting all cells from columns D through N inclusive for the X-input range, and column C for the Y-input range.

Using Stata to construct the dummy variables we type in the command

gen d1=0

replace d1=1 if country=="Colombia"

gen d2=0

replace d2=1 if country=="Bangladesh"

and so on for the five remaining countries, which means you will be excluding the United States from this operation. (Note that there is an easier way to program this in Stata, but I do not show it on purpose in order to reinforce the fact that there is a separate dummy variable for each country.) The Stata command line for running the regression then becomes

reg growth health health_sq inv pop d1-d7

and we get the output.

	Coef.	Std. Err.	t	P>|t|	[95% Conf. Interval]
Model	225.825354	11	20.5295776		F(11, 28) =	5.56
Residual	103.297482	28	3.6891958		Prob > F =	0.0001
					R-squared =	0.6861
					Adj R-squared =	0.5628
Total	329.122836	39	8.43904709		Root MSE =	1.9207

growth	Coef.	Std. Err.	t	P>|t|	[95% Conf. Interval]	
health	10.29633	6.789959	1.52	0.141	-3.61227	24.20493
health_sq	-.9779135	.4908819	-1.99	0.056	-1.983439	.0276125
inv	.4650919	.329233	1.41	0.169	-.2093113	1.139495
pop	2.345404	4.355408	0.54	0.594	-6.576244	11.26705
d1	-3.380077	3.475996	-0.97	0.339	-10.50033	3.740179
d2	13.48512	16.81666	0.80	0.429	-20.96224	47.93248
d3	-3.293638	1.712876	-1.92	0.065	-6.802305	.2150298
d4	6.775538	14.94551	0.45	0.654	-23.83895	37.39003
d5	2.740186	3.165811	0.87	0.394	-3.744685	9.225057
d6	14.94229	18.57023	0.80	0.428	-23.0971	52.98168
d7	1.200975	1.798921	0.67	0.510	-2.483948	4.885899
_cons	-34.0538	25.44829	-1.34	0.192	-86.18225	18.07465

Figure 2.8. Fixed effects regression.

The reader will notice that allowing each country to have its own intercept substantially changes the estimates of the other coefficients, and in particular, our marginal effect of interest. While the relationship between public healthcare spending and growth is still concave downward, the maximum is at a far larger percentage than it was. The new maximum is at a spending level of 5.269%. Therefore, not allowing the intercepts to differ produced substantial bias in our coefficient estimates. This sort of bias is called mean heterogeneity. (I won't go any further into this phenomenon here; just remember that it can substantially bias estimates if not addressed in the manner that we did.)

Now our inference is countries with spending levels below 5.269% will increase growth at a decreasing rate if they increase spending, and those with levels above this will increase growth by decreasing spending. Looking at our sample in Appendix 2.1, we find that this results in a clear dichotomy among our sample countries. One will notice that only the developing nations of Kenya, Colombia, Bangladesh, and Pakistan have health spending values at or below that amount, while the developed economies of the United States, United Kingdom, the Netherlands, and Italy all have values above that amount. In other words, developed countries can achieve higher growth if they reduce their spending while developing nations can attain higher growth rates if they increase their level of public healthcare spending.

Within Transformation

But what if we had 100 countries, do we construct 99 dummy variables? Well, we could, but that would be tedious. There's an easier way and it's called a *within transformation*. A within transformation allows one to run a "within" regression. Forget why it's called that, just remember that the outcome is the same as it is for constructing a separate dummy variable for each country.

What a transformation of this type does is take advantage of the fact that the dummy variables are time invariant for each country, allowing the researcher to effectively subtract them out of the regression before he/she runs it. We begin with equation (2.14) from earlier

$$y_{it} = a_{i0} + a_1 x_{it} + e_{it}. \tag{2.14}$$

Now, if we assume that this relationship is consistent over time, then we can rewrite (2.14) as

$$\overline{y}_i = a_{i0} + a_1 \overline{x}_i + \overline{e}_i, \tag{2.15}$$

where the bar across the top of each variable stands for that variable's time mean within country i. Now, subtracting (2.15) from (2.14), we get,

$$(y_{it} - \overline{y}_i) = (a_{i0} - a_{i0}) + a_1(x_{it} - \overline{x}_i) + (e_{it} - \overline{e}_i). \tag{2.16}$$

Since the constants do not vary over time, they cancel each other out, resulting in the equation

$$(y_{it} - \overline{y}_i) = a_1(x_{it} - \overline{x}_i) + (e_{it} - \overline{e}_i). \tag{2.17}$$

Hence, there is no need to construct dummy variables. We just transform the data as shown and we will get the same slope coefficient estimates as earlier. And since we are only interested in the a_1's anyway, we can still draw the inference needed to conduct our research. Just remember that (2.16) and (2.17) include *all* variables in our model, that is, Growth, Inv, Pop, and Health. So you must perform this transformation for all variables, you can't just do it for the Health variable.

Model Parsimony

One objective that all researchers want to achieve in their empirical work is model parsimony. Parsimony simply means frugality. In other words, we want the model we draw our final bit of inference from to be as small as possible without sacrificing our results. Therefore, we do not want to include irrelevant variables. An irrelevant variable is a variable which has a coefficient that is not statistically significant, does not affect the reliability of our results if taken out, or bias our results if taken out. An example of such a variable would be the squared healthcare spending variable, *but only if its coefficient was insignificant.* If this coefficient was insignificant, we could drop the variable from the model and proceed drawing inference from the linear form.

The linear version of that variable should *always* remain in the regression even if its coefficient becomes insignificant with the inclusion of the squared term. Reflecting on equation (2.15) we see that its coefficient, a_1, is the marginal effect's intercept. And even if it is not different from zero in a statistical sense, it is still not *actually* zero. Dropping this variable would be akin to dropping the intercept for the regression model itself. If we did that, the averaging line would be forced through the origin, artificially introducing a bias into our slope coefficient. Keep in mind, we should let the data tell us what the line should look like not the other way around; this applies to the marginal effect as well. Therefore, always keep the linear determinant of the quadratic form in the model even if its coefficient is insignificant. But what if we drop the squared health spending variable because its coefficient is insignificant, and the coefficient to the linear form is also insignificant, can we drop that one too? No, we can't drop the linear health variable even if its coefficient is insignificant after dropping the squared determinant. This is because it is our variable of interest. We wouldn't have anything to write about if we did. At some point, we determined that it would be interesting to see what effect public healthcare spending would have on growth; and if it has no effect on growth, that is interesting in itself—in other words, no results are many times as interesting as statistically significant results. In short, the protocol dealing with quadratic forms is this

1. If the coefficient of the squared form is insignificant, drop it.
2. If the coefficient is significant, keep it.
3. Always keep the linear form of that variable.

But what if the coefficients for the investment and population growth variables are insignificant, can we drop those as well?

With regard to the investment and population variables, remember the reasons why we included them in the first place. We included the investment variable for calibration and the population growth variable for theoretical omitted variable bias. And as mentioned earlier, the relationship between population growth, health spending, and economic growth may oppose one another and cancel out each other's effects. We were able to determine that including population growth did indeed change the inference we could draw from Health's marginal effect meaning that without its inclusion, bias did exist. Taking it out would reinstate bias into the model; so leave it in. The investment variable was included to calibrate the model, so like population growth, it had a specific function to perform. Hence taking it out would mean it could no longer perform that function; we would leave it in as well. To make a long story short, the final fixed effects model depicted in Figure 2.8 is indeed in the most parsimonious form possible.

Appendix 2.1. Panel Data For Chapter Examples

Year	Country	Growth	Inv	Pop	Health
2005	Colombia	3.142	19.659	1.532	5.289
2006	Colombia	5.070	21.333	1.511	5.199
2007	Colombia	5.327	22.091	1.487	5.105
2008	Colombia	1.241	20.861	1.461	4.928
2009	Colombia	−0.600	20.541	1.429	5.405
2005	Bangladesh	4.298	24.527	1.577	1.120
2006	Bangladesh	5.024	24.651	1.517	1.240
2007	Bangladesh	4.883	24.464	1.462	1.189
2008	Bangladesh	4.699	24.208	1.415	1.044
2009	Bangladesh	4.294	24.372	1.378	1.064
2005	Italy	−0.086	20.733	0.739	6.465
2006	Italy	1.457	21.094	0.569	6.563
2007	Italy	0.741	21.208	0.733	6.311
2008	Italy	−2.072	20.721	0.767	6.643
2009	Italy	−5.652	18.912	0.648	7.350
2005	Kenya	3.167	18.699	2.621	1.732
2006	Kenya	3.558	19.082	2.631	1.702
2007	Kenya	4.221	19.417	2.638	1.612

(Continued)

Appendix 2.1. (*Continued*)

Year	Country	Growth	Inv	Pop	Health
2008	Kenya	−1.094	19.717	2.642	1.537
2009	Kenya	−0.080	20.090	2.639	1.466
2005	Netherlands	1.808	18.897	0.234	5.946
2006	Netherlands	3.228	19.691	0.161	7.353
2007	Netherlands	3.388	20.107	0.218	7.320
2008	Netherlands	1.600	20.589	0.389	7.427
2009	Netherlands	−4.484	19.099	0.520	8.349
2005	Pakistan	5.103	17.461	2.411	0.699
2006	Pakistan	3.927	20.540	2.142	0.815
2007	Pakistan	3.443	20.923	2.142	0.793
2008	Pakistan	−0.557	20.451	2.142	0.850
2009	Pakistan	1.436	17.355	2.142	0.858
2005	United Kingdom	1.585	16.726	0.577	6.760
2006	United Kingdom	2.211	17.140	0.626	6.928
2007	United Kingdom	1.928	17.837	0.618	6.914
2008	United Kingdom	−0.151	16.595	0.697	7.156
2009	United Kingdom	−5.583	14.634	0.700	7.807
2005	United States	2.117	19.495	0.920	6.704
2006	United States	1.698	19.667	0.956	6.874
2007	United States	0.938	18.824	0.995	6.974
2008	United States	−0.919	17.708	0.923	7.259
2009	United States	−3.467	15.053	0.861	7.880

Suggested Reading

For deeper insight into fixed effects regression, one should read

Allison, P. D. (2009). *Fixed effects regression models.* Thousand Oaks, CA: SAGE Publications.

Baltagi, B. H. (2008). *Econometric analysis of panel data.* Chichester, UK: John Wiley & Sons, Ltd.

Green, W. H. (2003). *Econometric analysis.* Upper Saddle River, NJ: Prentice-Hall.

Hsiao, C. (2003). *Analysis of panel data (Econometric Society Monographs).* Cambridge, UK: Cambridge University Press.

CHAPTER 3

Basic Equation Editing and Table Design

In the previous two chapters we have seen several mathematical models displayed using Microsoft Word's equation editor. We have also seen several figures that depict the output of regressions we've run. In this chapter, you will learn how to construct these models and how to construct tables that are easy to understand, pleasing to the eye, and professional looking.

Equation Editing

Since economic research is grounded in mathematics, it is critical that the researcher be skilled in portraying the models in such a way that they give the reader a precise description of the type of data and the relationship being investigated. And while there are many different programs that allow one to construct equations, Microsoft Word (henceforth MS Word) is perhaps the easiest and certainly most widely used.

The program used to generate equations in MS Word is automatically built into the platform with Word versions 2007 and later. (Earlier versions will need you to physically add-in this feature.) With MS Word open, click on the Insert tab at the top and then on the down arrow button on Equation (this is an arrow just below the symbol π). There are several preprogrammed choices of equations, but instead click on Insert New Equation. A blue box will appear where your cursor is placed with the words inside the box Type Equation Here. Now there are two primary ways to construct your equation, by hand with the keyboard keys or using the buttons across the top. The former is the easiest.

Let us construct equation (3.1) from Chapter 2. This equation took the simple form

$$y_t = a_0 + a_1 x_t + e_t.$$ (3.1)

Inside the blue equation box that popped up, type the following:

$$y\_t=a\_0+a\_1$$

after the 1, tap the space bar, then follow with

$$x\_t+e\_t$$

and tap the space bar one more time. As you can see, the underscore tells the equation editor to make the next thing typed a subscript (that's why after the 1 you needed to tap the space bar or it would have made the x a subscript as well).

Now assume that you wanted to create an equation of the form (3.2) in Chapter 2 where there is a superscript and a subscript together on a variable, in this case on the x variable. This equation is of the form

$$y_{it} = a_0 + a_1 x_{it} + a_2 x_{it}^2 + e_{it} \qquad 3.2$$

So we would type

$$y\_it=a\_0+a\_1$$

and tap the space bar after the 1. Then continue with

$$x\_it+a\_2$$

and tap the space bar after the 2, and continue with

$$x\_it$$

tap the space bar, then type

$$\wedge2+e\_it$$

The ^2 right after tapping the space bar tells equation editor to place the superscript 2 at the top of the x.

The previous lesson on equation editing was only to get you started, but once you get through the lesson, you can play around with different symbols that can only be accessed by the buttons across the top of the equation editor interface. As you can see, an equation constructed in equation editor lets the reader decipher the relationships that are being tested, and also what type of data is being used from the subscripts connected with each variable. Now let's move on to tabling output which we haven't done yet.

Constructing Tables

The output portrayed in the figures in Chapters 1 and 2 were simply screenshots of Excel and Stata output tables. These *are not* what professionals use to embed into their research papers. In fact, in an undergraduate major capstone course I teach called Seminar in Economic Research, I issue a zero on the research paper of any student who uses cut and pasted Excel and/or Stata output tables in their papers. (I know that seems like an extraordinary policy, but I believe it is critical that my students know how to properly format a research paper.) A proper table for a research paper uses a proper tabling software package. You can of course use Stata's tabling commands to generate a table, but those commands are tedious to learn and not necessary. In my career as a researcher, I have always used MS Word's tabling software and have never had a reviewer, editor, or publisher reject or insist that I reformat my tables. That is the package we will use in our lesson below.

To insert a table into an MS Word document, simply place your cursor where you want the table, click the Insert tab, click on Table, and highlight the number of columns and rows you will need for your table. A couple of rules of thumb are needed here. The first is how many columns you'll need. Assume you are performing four permutations of the same regression—for instance, the simple linear form of regression (3) from Chapter 2, regression (3) itself, the same but with Inv included, and the same with Pop included. To table this output you will need five columns—one for each set of regression output and one for the variable list. Additionally, you will need five rows—a title row, a column header row, an output row, a descriptive statistic row that will include any additional statistical output such as the regressions' R^2, number of observations, number of countries, etc., and a row for notes to guide the reader on what is included in the table.

First, place the cursor where you want the table, and highlight 5 rows and 5 columns and you'll get something that looks like

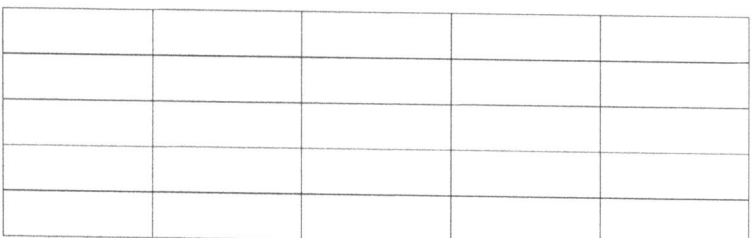

Figure 3.1. Example table unedited.

The boxes in this table are formatted for double-spaced sentences like yours may or may not be; regardless, the line spacing for each row will be whatever the line spacing is that is set for the paper proper. Whatever it is, wave your mouse arrow over the top left corner of the table until a plus sign appears and click on the plus sign. This will highlight the entire table. Standard line spacing for a table is single spacing. When the table is highlighted, change the line spacing like you normally would for any paper using the pull-down menu on the Home button bar. Your table should now look like

Figure 3.2. Example table with single spacing.

Once you've done this, it is normal to reduce the font of the table to 10-point font, even if your paper is 12-point font. To change the font, highlight the table once more and change the font just like you would for a paper. Your table will now look like

Figure 3.3. Example table 10-point font.

At this point, you are probably wondering how in the world do we fit all that output into this table? It's easy. First, we have to format the top row by merging cells and using the border options. Click on the uppermost left-hand cell in the table and drag to the right to highlight all the cells in the top row. Once highlighted, right click and click on Merge Cells. Then right click again and click on Borders and Shading. Once you click on Borders and Shading, a pop-up box will appear like in Figure 3.4.

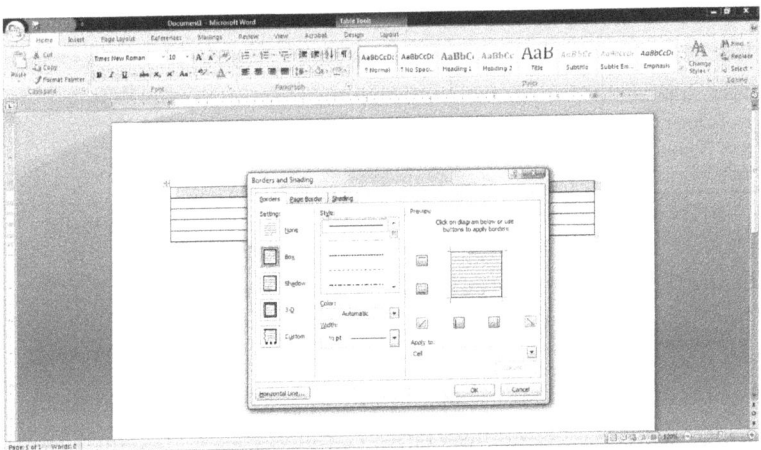

Figure 3.4. Borders and shading options.

In the Preview pane of the popup box, click once on all of the border lines except the bottom line, then click OK. You will notice that your table looks like it has lost the top row, but it really hasn't. Place your cursor where the first cell was and type "Table 1: Output for Growth Regressions." Also do the same for the bottom row, but this time delete all lines except the top line, and merge the cells as before, but don't write anything in it yet. Your table will then look like

Table 1: Output for Growth Regressions

Figure 3.5. Top and bottom lines formatted.

Next, fill in the necessary cells with the proper labels and notes until your table looks like

Table 1: Output for Growth Regressions

	1	2	3	4
Health				
Health Squared				
Inv				
Pop				
# of Observations # of Countries Adj. R^2				

Note: The dependent variable is real per capita GDP growth. * indicates significance at 10%, ** indicates significance at 5%. P-values are in parentheses.

Figure 3.6. Remaining rows and columns formatted.

The basic table construction is now complete. Having said that, the reader will notice a few things. First, the column labels are centered while the variable labels are justified left; this is common practice. Second, the note indicates that we will distinguish between 90% and 95% confidence intervals with regard to our p-values. * indicates that a coefficient is significant using a 90% confidence interval, while ** uses a 95% confidence interval. This sort of notation is commonplace. And lastly, there are two empty line spaces below each variable name. The reason we do this will be clear soon.

After entering the values of the coefficient estimates from the last chapter, our table will look like

Table 1: Output for Growth Regressions

	1	2	3	4
Health	-0.554 **	1.686 **	1.367	1.530 *
	(0.000)	(0.048)	(0.101)	(0.060)
Health Squared		-0.270 **	-0.215 **	-0.311 **
		(0.009)	(0.036)	(0.006)
Inv			0.338 *	0.070
			(0.061)	(0.747)
Pop				-2.213 *
				(0.056)
Constant	4.079 **	1.564	-5.282	4.921
	(0.000)	(0.184)	(0.163)	(0.439)
# of Observations	40	40	40	40
# of Countries	8	8	8	8
Adj. R^2	0.266	0.374	0.417	0.460

Note: The dependent variable is real per capita GDP growth. * indicates significance at 10%, ** indicates significance at 5%. P-values are in parentheses.

Figure 3.7 Coefficient estimates and p-values entered.

Even though our table appears to be complete, it isn't. We need to pretty it up so to speak using the Borders and Shading option (remember, highlight the cell of interest, then right click to find the Borders and Shading option). This option allows the researcher to embolden lines,

Table 1: Output for Growth Regressions

	1	2	3	4
Health	-0.554 **	1.686 **	1.367	1.530 *
	(0.000)	(0.048)	(0.101)	(0.060)
Health Squared		-0.270 **	-0.215 **	-0.311 **
		(0.009)	(0.036)	(0.006)
Inv			0.338 *	0.070
			(0.061)	(0.747)
Pop				-2.213 *
				(0.056)
Constant	4.079 **	1.564	-5.282	4.921
	(0.000)	(0.184)	(0.163)	(0.439)
# of Observations	40	40	40	40
# of Countries	8	8	8	8
Adj. R^2	0.266	0.374	0.417	0.460

Note: The dependent variable is real per capita GDP growth. * indicates significance at 10%, ** indicates significance at 5%. P-values are in parentheses.

Figure 3.8. Final table.

eliminate lines, turn single lines into double lines, etc. We will not go into the steps here for what I am about to do simply because each researcher has their own style for table formatting in this manner. But remember, don't get too artsy with it. You can easily turn an easy-to-read table into something that is a nightmare to read, greatly affecting the flow of the research paper. But, I would suggest that to start, you try your best to play around with the Borders and Shading option and try to duplicate the final table in Figure 3.8. This will allow you to become familiar with this program.

Suggested Reading

For more on how to use Microsoft Word for writing research papers, one should read

Kiernan, V. (2005). *Writing your dissertation with Microsoft Word: A step-by-step guide*. Alexandria, VA: Mattily Publishing.

Raubenheimer, J. (2013). *Doing your dissertation with Microsoft Word for academic writing: Updated for Microsoft Word 2007 and Microsoft Word 2010*. South Africa: True Insight Publishing.

CHAPTER 4

Choosing a Research Topic, Question, and Hypothesis

This chapter, true to its title, is about choosing a research topic, research question, and if warranted (or more importantly, if wanted), a research hypothesis. But first, we must define each, or better yet, explain what each is.

What Is a Topic, Question, and Hypothesis?

A research topic is the broadest area of economics for which someone has an interest. Being a globalization, growth and development economist, my topic area would be cross-country economic growth as I don't typically perform case study work involving only one country. For labor economists, their topic area would be a general field within labor, for instance, migration. For those interested in industrial organization, their topic area would be just that, a general area within industrial organization; perhaps it would be transfer pricing. Obviously then a research topic is that area that interests the researcher. On the other hand, a research question is more narrow and resides within the topic area.

If I were interested in economic growth volatility dissemination across countries, a research question I may want to evaluate might be "to what extent does growth volatility disseminate from developing to developed countries?" Another might be "does economic volatility affect growth rates in countries with high levels of foreign direct investment?" For a labor economist, one might ask "how does Hispanic migration affect the market for jobs in farming communities?" Another question may be "does the minimum wage affect unemployment in California?" It quickly becomes clear that a research question defines an issue of interest within the research topic. *It does not* place any prior conclusions on the outcome. In other words, a research question does not determine the direction of influence of the marginal effect on the left-hand-side variable; it only asks if a relationship exists, that is, is it a statistically significant relationship. On the other hand, a research hypothesis does exactly this.

A research hypothesis places what researchers call a *prior* to the research question. A prior is simply a belief that there will be a particular answer to the research question given common knowledge, or better yet, economic theory. Extending the volatility question posed above, a research hypothesis would be "we believe that economic volatility *negatively* affects growth rates in countries with high levels of foreign direct investment." A hypothesis within migration would be "we conjecture that Hispanic migration into the Midwest tends to *reduce* wages in the agricultural sector"; or "increases in the minimum wage *positively* affects the unemployment rate in California." Hypotheses can be even more specific than just a directional cause. For instance, one could presume that "developed countries, on average, disseminate approximately *one-third* of their growth volatility to developing countries." Having said that, today in economic research we normally don't go as far as placing actual values to our priors, we mostly just stick with direction of causation.

Choosing Each

While it's clear that a research hypothesis is a subset of a research question, and a question a subset of a research topic, choosing the question and hypothesis involves many more layers of consideration and deliberation. Choosing a topic area is easy, that is, it's simply a general area that interests a researcher. At this point, one doesn't need to consider any other factors. However, when choosing a question the researcher must determine (a) what type of paper he/she wants to write, (b) is the paper doable, and (c) is the question interesting to others and is it marketable?

What is meant by "type of paper" is whether or not the researcher intends to proceed to a hypothesis or not. While it's not intuitive that a researcher can write a paper that does not outline a hypothesis, it happens all the time and makes up a substantial portion of economic research. While many use different jargon, I will call a paper that doesn't formulate a hypothesis an *accounting* paper, and one that does an *explanatory* paper.

Imagine that two groups of researchers—call them groups A and B—want to estimate what the growth rate in real per capita GDP in Zimbabwe will be next year. Group A goes about this estimation by referring to economic theory and deriving a set of equations of investment spending, consumption spending, government spending, exporting, etc. They then empirically estimate each equation and solve the system simultaneously. In other words, this group derives equations that attempt to *explain* next period's growth rate.

On the other hand, group B simply relies on a purely empirical relationship relying on the fact that this period's growth rate is highly dependent upon what last period's growth rate was. This is a simple model with current growth on the left, last period's growth on the right side of the equation, and a regression is run. To estimate next period's growth they simply use the coefficient values obtained from this regression to project into the next period. But, there is no explaining of growth going on here. All Group B is doing is *accounting* for growth instead of trying to explain it. This example certainly highlights what an accounting paper is, but the prediction of next period's growth is a very specific case of an accounting paper. The vast majority of accounting papers are papers that simply stop at the research question and do not proceed to a hypothesis.

While many researchers may argue that accounting papers do not hold the same research value as explanatory papers, I would argue that it is exactly these accounting papers that further the science the most. For instance, if we were to wait on theorists to derive functional forms before any idea can be empirically tested, research in economics would still be stuck in the 1970s. There are many empirical economists out there with great questions to study that can tremendously further the science, yet they don't have the time and/or the expertise in that area to develop a formal theoretical argument before testing their idea. Furthermore, it may be the case that a hypothesis is premature at the time the idea is conceived and therefore no theoretical argument can yet be constructed. Accounting papers are also the primary type of paper written to test existing work! Many times a popular researcher's empirical work is flawed and someone (like me) comes along and tests their outcomes using better empirical techniques, discovers flaws in the existing work, and corrects them. Hence, it is exactly accounting papers that keep the research community from relying on flawed inference when developing policy.

The conclusion from this discussion is that an accounting paper typically doesn't have a hypothesis while an explanatory paper does. Therefore, an accounting paper also probably doesn't have any priors placed on outcomes while explanatory papers do. And while choosing a research topic area is probably easy, knowing this dichotomy between accounting and explaining helps significantly in determining whether to stop at the research question or move onto a hypothesis.

Regardless what you choose to do, it must be doable. Doability is key to any research. Doability in an accounting piece means that there is data available, or the data can be easily collected. Empirical methodology isn't as much of an issue because there exists a methodology out there that will model any form of data, even if imperfectly. But I have seen researchers waste months of valuable time trying to find or generate data that simply doesn't exist in a format that is conducive to answering the question.

Doability of a hypothesis means that the components of the hypothesis can be modeled in such a way that the integrity of the hypothesis remains unscathed. For instance, if one were to empirically model a production function of the form

$$y = l^a k^b, \tag{4.1}$$

an easy way to empirically test this relationship is to take the natural log of the equation to get

$$\ln(y) = a \ln(l) + b \ln(k). \tag{4.2}$$

Obviously, this can be empirically tested with a standard regression (just add an error on to the end). But what if the function were even more highly nonlinear? Getting the model into an empirically useful form and extracting the necessary information from algebraic manipulation may be problematic. And while an experienced researcher may be able to disentangle a model in such a way to effectively estimate it, it would likely be beyond the skills of someone just starting out.

The second criterion that one should meet when trying to come up with a question and/or a hypothesis is what I like to call the "who cares" factor. What I mean by this is that your question must be one that is interesting to others. Anyone can come up with a research agenda that is interesting to themselves. For instance, I may want to research exactly why my cats keep catching rodents off my property, yet insist on bringing them back onto my property for disposal. And while this question is interesting to me personally, I'm sure it wouldn't gain much traction as an interesting matter to the economics community at large.

And lastly, the research question and/or hypothesis should be marketable. I separate this from the "who cares" factor because an interesting question isn't always marketable. For instance, many gender-related or race-related issues are very interesting, but if you take on an issue that is highly controversial, it may not be a politically appropriate question to ask and therefore it would be difficult to get anyone to take your work seriously.

CHAPTER 5

Literature Reviews

Once you have selected your research question and/or hypothesis, you need to perform a literature review. A literature review is critical in answering the following questions:

1. What has been done on this topic?
2. Has anyone specifically addressed this question/hypothesis?
3. What are the typical empirical methodologies being used in this area?
4. What data sets are being used in this area (or does data even exist for it)?
5. If something has been done addressing this question/hypothesis, is there a way I can modify my idea to expand upon it, or are there flaws in the way the current literature approaches the question/hypothesis that I can address?

Just like the study of economics itself, performing a satisfactory literature review is as much of an art as it is a science. A poorly constructed literature review may lead the readers of your research to wonder if you are actually an expert on the subject, and whether they should trust what you are telling them.

Starting Off a Literature Review

The first thing *not* to do when starting a literature review is use a general web search engine, like Google. It is far too easy to start there as you can find anything anyone would want to know about any topic. The key to a good literature review is to only use peer-reviewed scholarly articles as your primary sources when researching your question; if needed use books and field-applied articles written by experts as secondary sources, and *never* use general topic newspaper articles, popular articles, blogs, opinion columns, etc., as any level of reference. Popular articles and opinions have not been thoroughly reviewed by researchers in the discipline before being published; therefore, their content may be questionable with regard to accuracy and/or integrity. Also, while books or separately articles from the Federal Reserve, National Bureau of Economic Research, World Bank, International Monetary Fund, etc., are written by well-known researchers and are quite useful for literature reviews, they should not be relied upon to provide the main support (or discredit) for your research question. This is because they are not peer-reviewed in the sense that they can be rejected for publication, hence they should only be used as a secondary means of reinforcement for your work.

You should always start a search by selecting the most dominant search engine in economics (or whatever field you are researching) which is EconLit. Your library should have access to EconLit's database. My library has EconLit with Full Text, which provides article access to over 500 journals in economics and economics-related fields. If you do not have access to a library or your library does not have access to EconLit, you (or the public) can log onto EBSCOhost and access EconLit through that (you may have to pay a fee for access).

Once logged into EconLit through your library's website (I'm not showing a screenshot of the actual interface because it might confuse the reader if their library uses a different interface to search EconLit), proceed to the Advanced Search area. In this area you will (most likely) find several blank lines separated by what are known as Boolean operators, and next to each line will be a pull down menu of field options. Boolean operators are connecting words such as "and," "or," and "not." "And" narrows a search, "or" expands it, and "not" excludes certain terms and therefore narrows the search as well. The operator "not" is rarely used when performing a literature review.

To search for an article, always use an abstract search. An abstract of a paper is simply a very brief (usually no more than 100–200 words) synopsis of the entire paper. A well-written abstract will include the research question, hypothesis if there is one, and most importantly, empirical inference drawn from the data work performed in the paper. And since the best in the business only become the best by writing good papers (and of course performing good research), all of your keyword search criteria should be contained in the paper's abstract. And this is key to performing a good search for literature—the keywords you use.

Combined with the Boolean operators, the keywords you use in your search are critical in determining how many hits you return with any search. In general, you probably don't want any more than 50 hits when all is said and done. I always start with the narrowest of searches using the Boolean operator "and." I fill in the first line with a word from the research topic area, and fill the next two lines with keywords pertaining to the research question (I always start with a three-line search).

Performing the Search

Let's start with the first question asked in Chapter 4. It was "to what extent does growth volatility disseminate from developing to developed countries?" The keywords I would start with in my abstract search would be

Growth

and

Volatility

and

Dissemination

Entering these into the EconLit interface provided by my library, I get only one hit—and it's my own paper!

This is clearly nowhere near the 50 I need. So, decidedly the word *dissemination* may be too original of a word to return enough articles. As an experiment, when I drop this word and rely only on *growth* and *volatility* (i.e., a two-line search), I get 2,114 hits; far too many to be useful. The best thing to do at this point is to replace the word *dissemination* with a more commonly applied word pertaining to the question.

Another common word for dissemination is *spillover*. Making this replacement and performing the search again, we get back exactly 30 hits. This may be all we need. This is because even though we are still 20 hits short of the 50 maximum, we can use the most recent articles in this search to expand our own search. Since all published research comes with its own literature review, we can use the work others have performed by researching the works they themselves have cited. So let's start perusing these 30 abstracts and see if any of them pertain to our research question.

48   A BEGINNER'S GUIDE TO ECONOMIC RESEARCH AND PRESENTATION

How to Gauge the Work

The very first abstract is

Figure 5.1. Abstract of paper for further review.

One can see that the title certainly refers to growth and volatility dissemination; and even though it is relegated to only G7 countries, the topic and general area within which our research question resides is spot on! So we keep this article for further evaluation. The second hit is

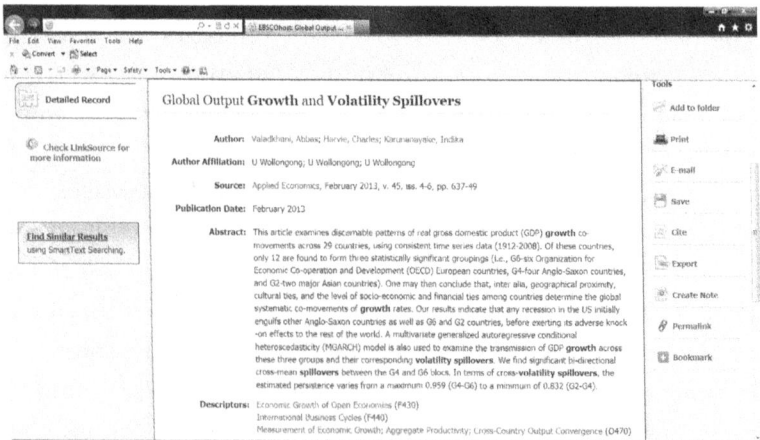

Figure 5.2. Another abstract of paper for further review.

which again is completely relevant to our own research topic and question. The third hit, however, is probably one we don't need to tag for further review.

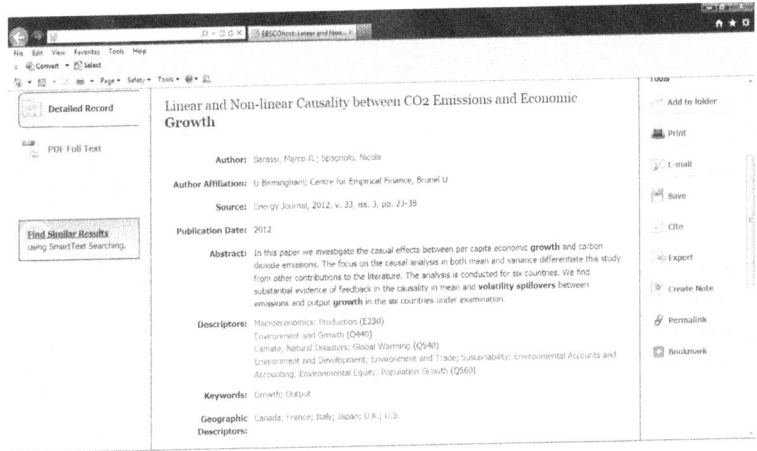

Figure 5.3. Abstract of paper to eliminate for review.

This paper has to do with causality and CO_2 emissions. Since our question asks "to what extent" does volatility spillover, it is purely an accounting research idea and is unlikely that emissions will have anything to do with it. Nevertheless, if after investigating each of the abstracts in this manner we only end up with 10 viable abstracts it may be necessary to go back and investigate marginal works such as this one.

Reading Selected Works

Once you have what you feel are enough papers to perform the literature review, you must eventually read them as well. Now to be honest, I don't personally know of a researcher who reads every paper word-for-word. That researcher may indeed exist (and this researcher is most likely an economics student doing their PhD dissertation), but I'm just not aware of such a person. However, you do want to read some of the papers thoroughly and others you should "meaningfully" skim through. By "meaningfully," I mean that a cursory glance is not good enough.

You should start by sorting the papers by quality of journal. There are many attempts at ranking journals out there all with their problems. I like to use a website called Research Papers in Economics, or RePEc for short (www.repec.org). This site lists journals according to their simple impact factor. I won't go into the details of what an impact factor is here, but roughly speaking an impact factor estimates the average number of citations that a typical paper in that journal will receive in any given year. In other words, it's a rough guide to how many times papers in that journal are used in other research, that is, how much *impact* does that journal have on the discipline. If you finally settle on, say, 30 papers to review, I would read word-for-word the 10 that are published with the highest impact factors according to RePEc. And that's easy enough; but how do we meaningfully investigate the other 20? There are some rules of thumb to follow here.

There are several sections of a paper that should always be read thoroughly: the introduction, the model and data section, and results section. The remainder of the paper can generally be ignored. These sections of the paper will typically make up about 50–70% of the entire paper, so you are not getting off scot-free, but you are substantially reducing the time it takes to perform the literature review.

For beginners and those not mathematically or econometrically inclined, when viewing the model section don't get bogged down in the details of the model itself. We have already covered what a basic regression setup is, and the subscripts attached to each variable will tell you all you need to know about the type of data being used (i.e., cross-sectional, time series, or panel). The verbal part of the model section will tell you all you need to know about the marginal effect(s) of interest. This section and the results section will also clue you into what other researchers are using for calibration and theoretical omitted variables.

For instance, a model out of one of my own research papers is shown below

$$V_{it} = a_{i0} + (D_N + D_{PR})\sum_{k=1}^{2} b_k V_{i,t-k} + D_R \sum_{k=1}^{2} c_k V_{i,t-k} + \sum_{k=1}^{2} d_k World\_V_{t-k}$$

$$+ \sum_{t=1}^{3} e_k X_{i,t-k-1} + D_N \lambda_N V_{jt} + D_{PR} \lambda_{PR} V_{jt} + D_R \lambda_R V_{jt} + r_{it}$$

This model may appear perplexing to some, but it is actually very easy to interpret if you simply look for the necessary information and not get bogged down in the details. To put this equation into context, Figures 5.4 and 5.5 are screenshots of partial pages 34 and 35 from "Evaluating Growth Volatility Susceptibility within Regional Free Trade Agreements" published in the *International Journal of Finance & Economics*, volume 16, in 2011.

The necessary information that explains the equation is all embodied in the text in each of the figures. It thoroughly, and in plain language,

$$V_{it} = a_{i0} + (D_N + D_{PR}) \sum_{k=1}^{2} b_k V_{i,t-k} + D_R \sum_{k=1}^{2} c_k V_{i,t-k} + \sum_{k=1}^{2} d_k \text{World_}V_{t-k} + \sum_{k=1}^{3} e_k X_{i,t-k-1} + D_N \lambda_N V_{jt} + D_{PR} \lambda_{PR} V_{jt} + D_R \lambda_R V_{jt} + r_{it} \quad (1)$$

The V_{it} in (1) stands for real per capita GDP growth volatility in country i at time t, while the V_{jt} stands for the trade-weighted average level of real per capita GDP growth volatility of the top ten trading partners for countries j at time t. The variable D_N is a dummy variable that equals one for countries that are not in any of the six agreements ASEAN Free Trade Area (AFTA), the Central American Common Market (CACM), the Central European Free Trade Agreement (CEFTA), the European Free Trade Association (EFTA), the G3 Free Trade Agreement (G3), and the North American Free Trade Agreement (NAFTA).[1] Two of the lesser agreements not mentioned here, and were largely impotent, would be the Latin American Free Trade Agreement, and the East African Customs Union mentioned in Krueger (1999); both of which were eventually disbanded. In addition, we do not investigate the Common Market for Eastern and Southern Africa because this agreement spans the entire period of our data set, which makes it impossible to differentiate between pre- and post-agreement results.

The variable D_R is a dummy variable that equals one for the countries that are currently engaged in one of the agreements, while D_{PR} is a dummy variable that equals one for those same countries but during years for which they are not actually engaged in the agreement. In other words, $D_{PR} = 1 - D_R$ for each of the countries listed in the six regional agreements.

Int. J. Fin. Econ. (2010)
DOI: 10.1002/ijfe

Figure 5.4. Screenshot of equation.

EVALUATING GROWTH VOLATILITY SUSCEPTIBILITY

We estimate (1) in two separate regressions using different specifications of the variable V_{jt}. The first type of V_{jt} is a weighted average of the top ten trading partners' volatility levels for only those trading partners *that are not involved in an RFTA*. The second form of V_{jt} includes volatility for countries *in an RFTA as well as those that are not* in an agreement. The former form allows us to quantify the effect of shocks that originate outside of the agreements' country list, while the latter form allows us to quantify the effect of shocks that originate from countries within the agreements' country list. The reader will notice that the second specification of the trade-weighted volatility variable includes trading partners that are in RFTAs as well as those that are not: the reason this variable does not consist only of RFTA countries is that there are only two RFTAs that include ten countries. Constructing the trading partner volatility variable with uneven country lists would necessarily require inconsistent weighting across groups. To this end, it will be more consistent to use the construction outlined above and to simply compare the results across volatility types. Furthermore, collinearity problems prohibit the inclusion of both types of volatility in the same regression—hence the reason for running two separate regressions.

From model (1), the coefficients of interest are λ_N, λ_{PR}, and λ_R, for each of the specifications of trade-weighted volatility.

For the first type of V_{jt}, a statistically significant and positive λ_N would indicate volatility spillover from trading partner economies that are not in an RFTA to economies that are also not in an RFTA. A significantly positive λ_{PR} would indicate volatility spillover from trading partner economies that are not in an RFTA to economies that are listed in an agreement, but currently are not engaged in an agreement. A significantly positive λ_R would indicate volatility spillover from trading partner economies that are not in an RFTA to economies that are currently engaged in an agreement.

Using the second type of V_{jt}, a statistically significant and positive λ_N would indicate volatility spillover from all trading partner economies to economies that are not in an RFTA. A significantly positive

Figure 5.5. Equation and variable description.

defines the dependent variable and the relationship(s) of interest. Just out of sight of these screenshots the paper defines the remaining right-hand-side variables, where they come from, and why their inclusion is important to the estimation of the equation (i.e., calibration and theoretical omitted variable bias). Hence, one can easily see that even though it appears intimidating, once you actually read the paper interpretation of these models is not an obstacle that can't be overcome.

CHAPTER 6

Data Collection and Formatting

In Chapter 2 we ran some regressions using data collected from the World Bank's World Development Indicators database. This data is freely available at www.worldbank.org. But it is only one of literally hundreds of databases available to the public for free. Obviously, what data you choose will be determined by your topic, question, and/or hypothesis. The novice researcher should keep several other factors in mind when searching for an appropriate data set to use for their empirical work: the type of data (time series, cross-sectional, panel; frequency of data collection), the accuracy of the data (who is it collected by; how is it collected), and the usability of the data (formatting data from one source; formatting data from multiple sources).

Type of Data

As we noted in Chapter 2, there are several types of data one would use for their research—time series, cross-sectional, and panel data. Again, the type of data will be determined by the area within which the research question lies. If you are interested in how inflation rates in the United States are affected by changes in domestic investment, using cross-sectional data would not work; the type of data you would collect for this investigation would be time series data, that is, observations of variables for the United States over time. In this instance you may want to visit the Federal Reserve Bank website at www.federalreserve.gov, where they have a data repository link. On the other hand, if you are interested in how investment affects inflation globally, you would want to collect panel data most likely from the World Bank or the International Monetary Fund. Regardless, the frequency of data collection is critical when using data with a time dimension, whether time series or panel data.

Since regression analysis involves generating an "average" relationship between two variables, obviously the more observations one has, the more that average will reflect the true empirical regularity in the data. Given that data with a time dimension is collected longitudinally, data that is collected every 3 months (i.e., every quarter in economic parlance) will supply more observations with which to estimate an average than will data that is collected every year. In our example above, World Bank data is only collected annually while most macroeconomic data for the United States is collected quarterly; therefore, domestically collected data would be optimal when researching a question involving just the United States to internationally collected data.

Since frequency of data collection seems to be critical, it behooves us at this point to address a couple of topics in this area. The first is having data that has too high of a collection frequency versus data that has too low of a collection frequency. For instance, stock price data can be collected in very small intervals—seconds and minutes, for instance. Some data, like international educational attainment data, may only be collected once every decade (say when a census is performed in a country).

Data collected at too high a frequency can result in problems with interpretation and inference once the regression is run. For instance, assume you are evaluating the relationship between two variables whereby observations are collected every 60 seconds. If the collection of one of the variables is even 30 seconds different from the other, can one be sure that the correlation between the two necessarily reflects the contemporaneous correlation? Furthermore, the amount of "noise" in the data itself, that is, since the variable changes every minute, may lead to empirical model specifications that are erroneous. I have personally noticed that a linear model fits high frequency data better than a nonlinear model; but using exactly the same data, a nonlinear model generates a better fit when that data is transformed to a lower frequency by averaging several observations over time.

So, what is the proper frequency of data to use? This is why modeling is really more of an art than a science. The research itself is science for sure, but modeling takes a lot of guess work and common sense thinking to perform correctly. The answer relies on what the researcher thinks is optimal for that particular level of research and the question being asked.

Holding the question itself constant, if the level of research does not require a high level of rigor, using lower frequency data is probably best as it can be easily modeled and inference is easier to digest.

Data that is collected at a very low collection frequency has its problems as well. First, data that is collected say, every 10 years, only gives a brief snapshot of the variable at one point in time—every 10 years. What happens to that variable in between these times is anyone's guess. Take population growth, for instance. If only census data were to be used for population growth rate purposes, one might find a dramatic decrease in growth rates from the 2000 census to the 2010 census using prior decades as reference points. But did that decrease start in 2001, 2002, 2005, or 2009? No one knows. Low frequency data is even more of an issue when you try matching this type of data up with higher frequency data. In my own work I consistently use right-hand-side variables that are collected every 5 years, but then have other right-hand-side variables as well as left-hand-side variables that are collected every year! The problem with the interpretation of the results in this case (drawing inference) is obvious.

To me, a rule of thumb is to use quarterly data for most time series purposes. For cross-sectional and panel data that is collected for developed countries, use annual data if available—and it usually is. For developing country data take as high a frequency as one can get. Much developing country data is gathered sporadically at best; in other words, there may be a continuously collected series of data, but one that has large gaps in it for several years at a time. Therefore, even though it is continuously collected, it isn't consistently collected. When modeling data that has large gaps in it, it is critical that the researcher appropriately matches up the time dimension across variables if this occurs. You don't want to match up the observations of one variable that was collected annually between 1976 and 1983 with those of another variable that was collected annually between 1987 and 1990.

The Accuracy of the Data

Data accuracy has been, currently is, and always will be a controversial topic in the world of empirical research—and rightly so. However, someone once said "don't let perfection get in the way of progress" (who that was, I have no clue). The idea that there exists a data set that doesn't have some reliability issues is nonsense. This means that we work with what we have to the best extent we can, and draw whatever inference is possible given the data we have. So what is the most practical way to deal with flawed data?

Frankly in some circles the flaws in data are simply ignored. Not in the sense that researchers in those area(s) don't realize the flaws, but that everyone knows the data has reliability issues; if the issues are common knowledge, there is no real need to explain them every time research is conducted using that data set. In this sense, there is effectively a permanent and unspoken caveat placed on all inference drawn using that data.

Developing country data and data collected by survey tend to have these sorts of issues. In the former case, agencies such as the World Bank, IMF, United Nations, etc., must rely on governments to provide them with their data. Many times it isn't in the government's best interest to let the world know about high inflation in its economy and therefore will report inflation numbers that are below the actual levels. Or a country may not want the international community to know that their poverty rate is as high as it actually is, and therefore will purposely under report these figures. In the latter case, reliability issues are a result of human nature. Survey questions, if not properly formatted and executed in such a way to avoid swaying the opinion of the respondent, can lead to substantial bias in the responses. Everyone in the research community knows this and naturally proceeds with caution when drawing inference from survey data.

Developed country data is less problematic than developing country data because of the checks and balances across different government agencies and the pressure from the private sector to produce accurate data. However, this data is mostly collected using sampling which of course is prone to error. This is why, for instance, United States quarterly GDP numbers, unemployment numbers, or most all economic numbers for that matter, are updated two to three quarters after they are reported. It may take this long for more data to come in that would require a readjustment of the numbers reported in the past.

DATA COLLECTION AND FORMATTING 57

Usability of the Data

Data sets can come in many formats. And depending on the type of empirical work you wish to perform, loading your data can take a lot of time and effort. But it can't be emphasized enough that spending this time making sure your data is formatted and loaded properly will save the researcher a lot of headache and much embarrassment in the long run.

Regressions are performed using data for variables that are in columnar format. These columns are called *vectors*. Therefore, if you are performing time series regressions, the variable labels should be at the top of each vector, and subsequent rows should contain observations for that variable over time. For cross-section work, the variable labels will still be contained in the top row, while the subsequent rows contain observations for each individual/country. For empirical work using panel data, each individual/country will have a time dimension in subsequent rows. Figure 6.1 shows examples of each using the data from Chapter 2.

The reader will notice how the cross-section format does not include a vector labeled "Year." This is because cross sections have no time dimension that is necessary for the regression itself. This is not to say that the period for which the cross-sectional data was collected isn't important—it is and should be reported in the research. It's simply not necessary for

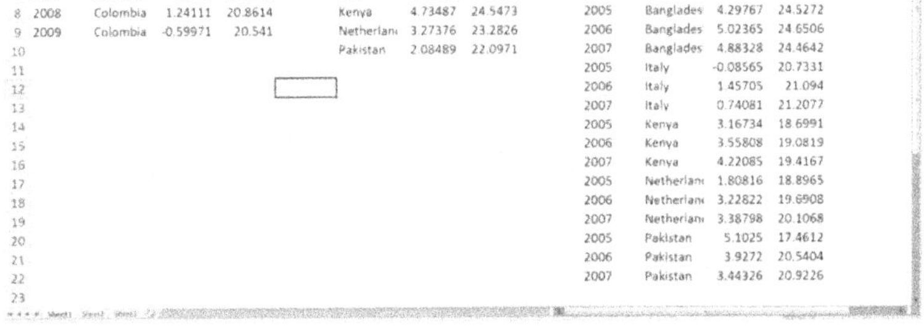

Figure 6.1. Examples of data types.

formatting data for regression analysis. (In this particular example, the reader will also notice that each cross section observation is simply the time mean of the panel observations for each country.)

To make a long story short, your data set should look exactly like one of those mentioned above before you run any regressions! This is easy, right? Not always. In many instances, the researcher may need to perform a task called *merging* that blends data attained from one source with that of another source. It may be the case that the years for one variable do not always match up with those of another. And while this problem can exist with all three types of data in Figure 6.1, I will address these issues reflecting only on the panel data set since it is essentially the union of the time series and cross-section sets.

Assume we have two variables for a set of countries as in Figure 6.2. You will notice that the years for these two variables do not match up with each other. Specifically, in the left-hand columns, one finds that the growth variable has observations for each country for years 2005–2008, but the investment variable only has observations for years 2006–2009. Since regression packages cannot recognize missing observations (try running a regression using this data), we must actually drop the entire row within which the missing observation exists. While nearly all regression packages, including Stata, will automatically drop these missing observations when the regression is performed, I still like to purge the data first

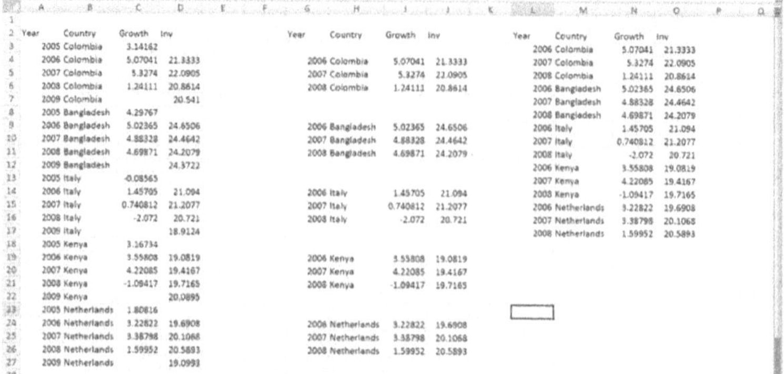

Year	Country	Growth	Inv
2005	Colombia	3.14162	
2006	Colombia	5.07041	21.3333
2007	Colombia	5.3274	22.0905
2008	Colombia	1.24111	20.8614
2009	Colombia		20.541
2005	Bangladesh	4.29767	
2006	Bangladesh	5.02365	24.6506
2007	Bangladesh	4.88328	24.4642
2008	Bangladesh	4.69871	24.2079
2009	Bangladesh		24.3722
2005	Italy	-0.08565	
2006	Italy	1.45705	21.094
2007	Italy	0.740812	21.2077
2008	Italy	-2.072	20.721
2009	Italy		18.9124
2005	Kenya	3.16734	
2006	Kenya	3.55808	19.0819
2007	Kenya	4.22085	19.4167
2008	Kenya	-1.09417	19.7165
2009	Kenya		20.0895
2005	Netherlands	1.80816	
2006	Netherlands	3.22822	19.6908
2007	Netherlands	3.38798	20.1068
2008	Netherlands	1.59952	20.5893
2009	Netherlands		19.0993

Year	Country	Growth	Inv
2006	Colombia	5.07041	21.3333
2007	Colombia	5.3274	22.0905
2008	Colombia	1.24111	20.8614
2006	Bangladesh	5.02365	24.6506
2007	Bangladesh	4.88328	24.4642
2008	Bangladesh	4.69871	24.2079
2006	Italy	1.45705	21.094
2007	Italy	0.740812	21.2077
2008	Italy	-2.072	20.721
2006	Kenya	3.55808	19.0819
2007	Kenya	4.22085	19.4167
2008	Kenya	-1.09417	19.7165
2006	Netherlands	3.22822	19.6908
2007	Netherlands	3.38798	20.1068
2008	Netherlands	1.59952	20.5893

Year	Country	Growth	Inv
2006	Colombia	5.07041	21.3333
2007	Colombia	5.3274	22.0905
2008	Colombia	1.24111	20.8614
2006	Bangladesh	5.02365	24.6506
2007	Bangladesh	4.88328	24.4642
2008	Bangladesh	4.69871	24.2079
2006	Italy	1.45705	21.094
2007	Italy	0.740812	21.2077
2008	Italy	-2.072	20.721
2006	Kenya	3.55808	19.0819
2007	Kenya	4.22085	19.4167
2008	Kenya	-1.09417	19.7165
2006	Netherlands	3.22822	19.6908
2007	Netherlands	3.38798	20.1068
2008	Netherlands	1.59952	20.5893

Figure 6.2 Formatting with unbalanced time dimension.

to actually see the usable period(s) covered by it. This way, I can adjust the inference I make from the results as needed.

Suggested Reading

Stengel, D. N., & Chaffe-Stengel, P. (2011). *Working with economic indicators: Interpretation and sources*. New York, NY: Business Expert Press.

Heeringa, S. G., West, B. T., & Berglund, P. A. (2010). *Applied survey data analysis*. Boca Raton, FL: Chapman and Hall/CRC.

CHAPTER 7

Drafting and Refining the Paper

A famous economist named David Romer once outlined a detailed plan of how PhD students could graduate in 5 years or less. The plan goes something like this (from Brad DeLong's website http://www.j-bradford-delong.net/teaching_folder/Romers_rules.html)

- Don't clutter up your life with other activities; just write
- Don't carry out a thorough and comprehensive search of the literature; just write
- Don't attempt to make sure that every page you write shows the full extent of your professional skills; just write
- Don't write a well-organized, well integrated, unified dissertation; just write
- Don't think profound thoughts that shake the intellectual foundations of the discipline; just write
- If you don't have a paper started by the spring of your third year, be alarmed
- If you don't have a paper largely drafted by the fall of your fourth year, panic
- Have three new ideas a week while you are getting started
- Don't try to game the profession, work on what interests you
- Good papers in economics have three characteristics
  - A viewpoint
  - A lever
  - A result

The point here is that when drafting a good research paper, get something down in writing quickly even if significant flaws are found during revisions.

A good paper goes through many, many drafts before it is ready to be presented to an interested audience. I've published dozens of journal articles, and there is not one paper that hasn't been revised at least 15 times before sending it to a journal for review. Up to this point in the book, you now have the skills to perform basic regression analysis, format equations and tables, decide on and find a topic/question/hypothesis, collect and format data sets, and perform literature reviews; in other words, you have the basic skills needed to start drafting your paper. In this chapter, we will lay out standard paper format settings and tips in drafting and revising your paper.

Paper Formatting

One of the most popular, and personally preferable font sizes is 12-point font. To me, Times New Roman is the easiest to read although some may disagree. Another easy-to-read font is 12-point Arial; like Times New Roman, it is also quite popular. What a writer does not want to do is create undue stress on the reader with something as minor as font size and type. Hence, if the writer chooses one of these two fonts, the reader will enjoy the read provided, of course, that the content is interesting.

Line spacing and the justification of text are also important. With draft papers, double-spaced lines are preferred. Not only is double-spaced text easy to read, but someone reading the draft may want to make notes, highlight or underline parts of the text, or take part in some other notational scribbling. Having a large space between lines helps the reader with these tasks.

Justification is how the script is aligned on the page. There are four justification alignments—left, right, middle, and both sides. In MS Word's tool bar across the top of the page, in the Paragraph box, one will find these four justification buttons. Left justification aligns all the text on the left-hand side of the page, while right-hand justified text aligns it on the right. Centered text does exactly that; it lets the text fall where it wants to on the left and right sides, but centers it in the middle of the page.

I personally prefer text that is justified on both sides. This type of justified text does sometimes leave large gaps within sentences depending on where long words fall at the end of a line, but looks much cleaner overall and is very easy on the eyes. Furthermore, justification on both sides is the most common format that journals use for published papers. Therefore, using this justification type gives one a fairly good idea of how their paper would look when presented to the general public. You should also note that formatting multiple columns on a single page is not generally acceptable in research regardless of justification—leave this to newspapers and some journals.

The next big formatting issue when drafting a research paper is the title page. A title page should be neat, concise, yet give a large amount of information about the paper. It will include the title of the paper, author list with the lead author first (i.e., the most important author to that piece—usually the one who came up with the research idea to begin with), abstract, JEL codes, keywords, and in the footnote of the page, contact information for the corresponding author (this may or may not be the lead author). In other words, it should look like Figure 7.1.

From the top of Figure 7.1, you will notice that the title is centered on the page and is single line spaced if it takes up more than one line. It is also about a fifth to a quarter of the way down the page from the top. How far down depends on the size of the abstract. Next we have the author list; it is also single spaced. The word "by" in between is optional, but I believe including it is more formal than not. Underneath the author list is a single-line-spaced abstract that, as mentioned earlier, should summarize the research question and/or hypothesis, as well as a brief description of the inference drawn from the empirical work. Below the abstract are the JEL and keyword lists.

JEL stands for Journal of Economic Literature. The JEL Classification Codes Guide can be found on the American Economic Association's website at www.aeaweb.org. The JEL codes are simply descriptors with which audiences classify research topic and question areas within the field of economics and related fields such as finance. The first letter of a JEL code describes the topic area. The letter F, for instance, is the topic area of international economics. Digging deeper, one may want to study globalization as it relates to international economics; then one would add the number 6. Therefore, globalization within the context of international economics would be F6. Now assume you wanted to study how globalization affects labor movements from developing to developed nations; this would be in

64   A BEGINNER'S GUIDE TO ECONOMIC RESEARCH AND PRESENTATION

>   Title Should Go Here Centered in Page and About One-Quarter to One-Third of the Way Down the Page
>
>   by
>
>   Jeffrey A. Edwards[1]
>   Second Author
>   Third Author
>
>   Abstract:..
>   ....
>   ....
>   ....
>   ....
>
>   JEL Codes: 3 codes is sufficient
>   Keywords: 3 to 5 keywords is sufficient
>
>   [1] Contact information for corresponding author. Affiliation and Department................., Email:................,
>   Address:............................., Phone:.........................

Figure 7.1. Title page formatting.

sub area 6. Hence, the complete JEL Classification Code for this research question would be F66. Generally, two additional codes would be listed as well. These would be codes that may not describe the research as precisely as F66, but focuses on an area in the paper which is related to that particular piece of research.

The keywords are used to construct easily searchable descriptors for engines such as EconLit. Therefore, the keyword chosen as well as the number of keywords is critical in affecting the number of people that find your paper when they do a search. I generally provide four or five keywords. But, at the minimum you should have at least three. Out of these three one should address the topic, the question, and the empirical method used such as fixed effects modeling. Notice how this last keyword is actually a phrase. There is no rule for keywords being single words, or short phrases; but if you use a phrase as one of your keywords, keep it very short and distinct.

Construction and Contents After the Title Page

After the title page, you should construct the paper as follows. Introduction, literature review (sometimes combined with the introduction if the paper is relatively short), a model and data section, results section, discussion section (many times included in the results section; this is where general inference is applied directly to the question/hypothesis), conclusion, and at the end, a references section. (I'm ignoring any appendices that may be needed for the paper.) Each section of the paper should have the headings as listed (e.g., the literature review section should be titled "Literature Review"), although some discretion can be used if the context of the paper requires it.

Each of the section headings should be in bold type. *Never* put the section headings in a font size that is more than two sizes larger than the main text. For instance, if your main text is 12-point font, do not use any font size larger than 14-point font for the section header. I generally just keep them the same size. Also, do not use type that is different from the rest of the text. If your paper is in Arial font, your section headers should also be in Arial font.

Below the section headers, the first paragraph should *never* be indented. The purpose of an indent is to start a new idea—and that's what the header already does. Therefore, there is no need to indent the first sentence of the first paragraph under the headers. Start indentations with the second paragraph. And finally, there is the references section to talk about.

References are extremely important in order to give credit where credit is due. I won't go into all of the arguments and details outlining plagiarism, your instructor can cover that in person, but always reference when in doubt; in other words, always err on the side of too many references, not too few. There are no real consequences for having too many references, but there are for having too few.

There are two types of referencing that occur in every paper—in-text citations and referencing those citations at the end of your paper. The standard format for an in-text citation is to use brackets with authors' last name(s) and year of publication. Figure 7.2 shows a screenshot of a draft version of one of my own papers.

Some researchers prefer to use parentheses rather than brackets. And truthfully, whichever you use is up to you. I personally prefer brackets for in-text citations as they make a clear distinction for the reader between what is a citation, and what is an extension of an idea. Having said that, the references section at the end of the paper has a format of its own.

The references section is a stand-alone section that elaborates on the in-text citations to include not only author names, but journal title, volume number, issue number, publication date, and pages within which the article resides. The problem is that the preferred format of the references contained in the references section is different for everyone. But there are some standards to follow.

Citation styles seem endless. I won't go into all of them here, but one guide written by Kate L. Turabian (http://www.press.uchicago.edu/books/turabian/turabian_citationguide.html) is a good start. In general,

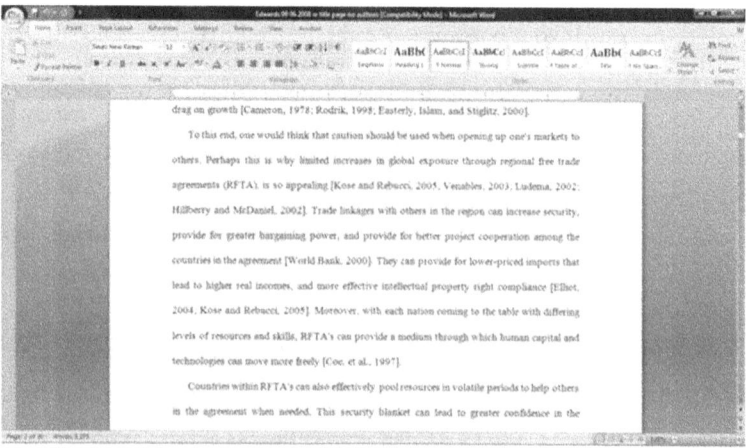

Figure 7.2.

for research papers you start with the author's last name first, then first name and middle initial. Lead author always goes first. Then the title of the journal, volume and issue numbers, year published, and pages in that journal where the article can be located. For books it is slightly different, but similar. Regardless of the style you choose, the bottom line is this: include all the information in the reference that would be necessary to easily locate the manuscript if someone wanted to. The reason why I am more concerned about the content of the citation rather than its actual construction is simply because I've found that, once again, every journal and researcher is different with regard to styles. I've even sent articles to journals that stipulated a particular citation style in their own style guide, only for the article to be returned to me from the galley proofers requesting that I change the style to something completely different! Therefore, to me content is far more important than style.

The Drafting Process

When initially drafting a paper, follow Romer's guide mentioned above—just write. Get your thoughts down on paper. It's the revisions that matter most anyway. Having said that, at this point in the drafting process be careful not to attempt to copy the prose of existing published material to the extent that you are "trying to sound like the experts." Remember that these are experts in their respective areas and can string together words and ideas that make perfect sense (or not) within the research community at large. You must face the fact that you are not at that level yet. Keep your sentences simple, concise, and accurate, but in your own words.

A good paper is revised somewhere between 10 and 20 times before the final product is packaged for public consumption. It seems like a lot of revisions and it is. But most people that think less is needed are probably not finding all the flaws they should during the revision process. This is because there exists a phenomenon whereby someone that reads their own work over and over again tend to read the words but not read the context within which the words lie. Furthermore, many will see the first few words of a sentence they know by heart and not read the rest of the sentence. You would be amazed how many flaws I've found in my writing on the 6th or 8th time reading the same sentence! In general, there are some protocols to follow.

The first few readings of your draft involve two things—accuracy and accuracy. I mention this twice to emphasize the point that inference you draw on empirical work the first time may not be correct. Go back over your models, results, and most importantly, the inference you draw from your results many times. It would be quite embarrassing to rely on incorrect inference when the audience knows better. Accuracy also includes making sure that the literature review you conducted actually pertains to the question at hand. In reviewing other's work over the years, you would be astounded how many authors cite work that has absolutely nothing to do with their research question.

The next few readings of your draft should focus on starting to "tighten things up" if you will. This reading should include looking for typos, sentence structure, formatting issues, flow, etc. *Do not* depend on MS Word's spell and grammar checks. Do it yourself! At this stage, if you don't know how to write a proper sentence, use the appropriate words, or look up how a particular word is spelled, you should seek help from someone that does—but not a computer! Don't be ashamed to have others proofread your work or give advice. No one starts off their life writing well; learning to do so requires experience writing and external proofreaders. After a while you will start writing better and better, then before you know it you'll need the proofreaders less and less. But this all takes time and many papers—it doesn't happen overnight and it will never happen if you depend upon a computer to catch and evaluate your mistakes. A caveat, however. Many are accustomed to writing in a *creative* way from an English or literature class. Creative writing *is not* research writing. So just make sure your proofreaders are also researchers.

The last item, flow, is critical. If your paper doesn't flow well the audience will become confused and frustrated. If this happens you'll lose them very quickly. What is flow? It's the idea that the reader should not get confused when reading your paper. Assume you have a paper addressing how investment affects economic growth. You write three paragraphs in the introduction to that effect. But then out of nowhere you include a paragraph about how the sun heats up the earth. Afterward you go back to the original research question. In this extreme example, the reader would probably be confused as to why you included that paragraph within the context of growth and investment. This would break the flow of the read and greatly irritate the person reading your piece.

Fine Tuning

The last stage is what I call the "fine tuning stage" of paper revision. In this stage you literately read the *entire* paper word-for-word, line-by-line. This is where you put the finishing touches on the paper; but it is also the phase that takes the most time. Not because you necessarily read it more slowly (although I do), it's because the most effective way to fine tune a paper is to read it, revise it, and put it down for a while! I will usually read it over and fine tune it once a day, every day, for a series of days. Having a large gap between readings helps you in finding that "piece of the puzzle you weren't able to find before." If you've ever put together a large jigsaw puzzle, you always run into that missing piece you can't seem to find. You cuss, you throw things, you yell at your spouse, but ultimately it's time away from the puzzle that works the best. You find that if you put the puzzle down for a couple of days you come back and the piece jumps out at you. The final revision of the paper should be conducted in the same way.

In the end, the paper should be perfect with regard to readability and formatting. Of course, someone (in particular the editors of the publishing house) will always change something you've done, but in general the paper is perfectly formatted, all references are included, the paper makes sense, is fun to read, and flows well!

CHAPTER 8

Pointers on Presenting to a Live Audience

By now you have finished your paper and are ready to present it to a live audience—probably your class and/or instructor. Presenting material to an audience is not easy. It not only takes confidence in your work, which this book can't teach you, but also brevity, flexibility, and knowledge. This chapter will give you some pointers when presenting your material to others. What it will not do is teach you how to relax and avoid stage fright; no book can teach you that. Only practice will give you the ability to present in a calm, deliberate way. However, these pointers will certainly help you enhance your presentation style and hopefully make you feel more comfortable as you present your material.

Constructing Slides

I won't go into the actual construction of slides such as PowerPoint slides, or slides generated in other media. Most of those programs are fairly straightforward to use, but unlike Microsoft Word, Microsoft Excel, or Stata, slide construction software mostly require playing around with them to get skilled at using them. But what I will cover is how to construct a slide in such as way as to be informative and appeal to the audience without confusing or boring them.

The vast majority of presenters are allowed no more than 20 minutes to present their research. Many of the conferences I've attended allow only 15 minutes. So exactly how does one present a substantial piece of research in that short a time frame? There are some rules of thumb to follow in achieving this objective.

The first three pointers are (a) don't make too many slides, (b) keep the number of slides you make low, and (c) make a small number of slides. Of course, all three of these pointers say the same thing. That's because making too many slides is perhaps the biggest fault anyone has when new at presenting to an audience. A rule that I have kept to that works well is one slide for every 2 minutes of presentation—and this includes the title slide! This means that a 20-minute presentation should have no more than 10 slides; a 15-minute presentation should only have 7 to 8 slides—again, this includes the title slide. Newly minted PhDs in economics are the worst offenders. I've seen presenters come to conferences with files containing 30 and 40 slides, knowing that they only have a 20-minute interval to present this material. This means that a presenter would have to cover 2 slides per minute! An impossible task. And while many may not see a problem with only getting through part of the material, it makes you look incompetent, unknowledgeable, and simply lacking any intuition whatsoever. So exactly how does one present so much material on only 8 or 10 slides? It's actually quite easy.

At first, a knee-jerk reaction would be to cram in as much material on each slide as you can. But this is exactly what you *don't* want to do. If you have more than 4 to 5 bullet points on each slide, you have too many. The key is to *know your material and know it well*. If you know your material like the back of your hand, it is easy to show a bullet point and elaborate on it without actually having the text on the projector screen. But this task requires something that many new researchers simply don't, or can't, do—that is, to turn around and face the audience; in other words, actually speak to the audience and not the slide.

Addressing the Audience

All of you as students in the modern age have had instructors that simply regurgitate Microsoft PowerPoint slides from the textbook. Ask yourself this question: how much did I actually learn? Relative to staying home and reading the book, probably not much. And this is because instructors that do this are not interacting with their audience, that is, you students. Slides have no personality, and no knowledge of the material; in fact, slides are inanimate objects. They can't think, speak, elaborate on subject matter, etc. Therefore, instructors that don't do this, by definition, are thinking, speaking, and elaborating on the subject matter. But they can only do this if they actually *know* their subject matter.

I never use slides in the classroom. My personal opinion is that if the instructor cannot simply write the topic on the board and turn around to the class and improvise the remainder of their lecture, then why did they get an advanced degree in the area? Why did they waste their time? They certainly didn't learn anything in graduate school. Students are amazed when I go into my lectures with only one or two pages of notes, and on those pages are simply topic outlines. I can do this and be far more effective in my teaching because I know my subject matter like the back of my hand—I do have a PhD after all and should be an expert in my area! And this is exactly the way you should think about the presentation of your own material. If you are an expert in your particular area, you shouldn't need detailed slides from which to present your material; just brief notes will be sufficient.

Length of Presentation

Figure 8.1 is a good example of a slide presentation with enough material to inform the audience, yet not too much to be hard to read and interpret. These are screenshots of an actual set of slides I presented to the 2008 conference of the Missouri Valley Economic Association. I use screenshots here to show the reader exactly how the slides will appear on the projector. There are not any pretty colors or watermarks on them, just basic slides. This reflects the fact that I am a traditionalist. You have material to present, not artwork. Having said that, how much artwork you put on your slide is up to you and I have certainly seen presentations with very nice slide backgrounds that do enhance the presentation. Just be careful. I've also seen slides whereby the presenter has gone overboard with regard to the artistry of their slides actually affecting their readability—don't fall into that trap.

One can see that I have summarized all of the primary areas of my research paper—the introduction, literature review, model section, results section, and conclusion. Nothing is missed, and all in only seven slides (the actual length of this draft paper was 26 pages). Furthermore, the audience can almost tell exactly what the work is about without actually listening to my presentation simply because the slides are also informative.

Structural Assimilation with Trading Partner Economies

Jeffrey A. Edwards
(School affiliation goes here)

MVEA 2008

Introduction

- As Developed economies have "developed", their private and policy-making sectors have acquired the ability to exploit growth in the rest of the world, while to some extent insulating themselves from external shocks.

- What we ask here is whether this same type of structural effect is happening with developing countries.

- Our results indicate that structural assimilation in growth has occurred among Emerging markets, while assimilation in volatility has occurred among Developing countries.

Literature Review

- Conley and Ligon (2002), Weinhold (2002), Arora and Vamvakidis (2005), Castilleja-Vargas (2007), Akin and Kose (2007): On average, findings show a positive trading partner economy correlation of .65%.

- Kose, Prasad, and Terrones (2003a,b), Gruben, Koo, and Millis (2002): business cycles synchronize as trade increases.

- Imbs (2004), Shin and Wang (2003), Barnett and Mehmet (2007): structural implications of business trade synchronization.

Figure 8.1. Continued.

POINTERS ON PRESENTING TO A LIVE AUDIENCE 75

Model

- Primary model:

   (1) $y_{it} = a_0 + a_1 y_{it-1} + a_2 y_{it-2} + a_3 y_{jt} + e_{it}$

Coefficient of interest is a_3 over time.

- 5-year rolling window method that starts in 1982.

- Developed Economies, Emerging Economies, and Developing Economies are used.

4

Figure 1: Rolling Window GMM Estimates of Growth Spillovers

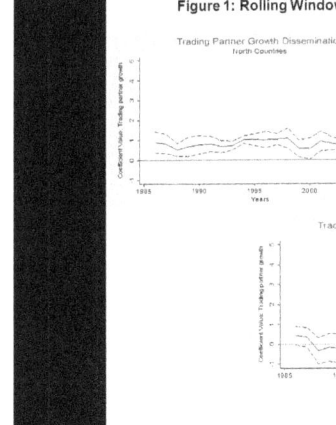

5

Figure 2: Rolling Window GMM Estimates of Volatility Spillovers

6

Figure 8.1. Continued.

Conclusion

- The structural assimilation involving economic growth dissemination between Emerging economies and Developed economies has been more apparent over time, and the same is true for Developing and Developed economies with regard to growth volatility.
- Therefore, it appears that Developing economies are becoming more like Developed economies, i.e., the public and private sectors are structurally assimilating to absorb trading partner shocks.
- This may be due the standards that the Developing countries must meet to benefit from transfer payments and lending reliance on Developed nations.

Figure 8.1.

One additional point I will make with regard to constructing your presentation is font size. Remember that what you see on your computer screen you see at a distance of about one to two feet. However, the audience will be at a far greater distance. Make sure that you have large enough font that the audience has an easy time reading your slides. My titles are generally around 40-point font size while the body material uses around 24-point font size. This may seem large, but as an experiment construct your slides using smaller font, project them onto a screen, then stand back about 25 to 30 feet from the screen and you'll see what I mean—they start to become difficult to read at that distance.

Suggested Reading

Paradi, D. (2010). *102 tips to communicate more effectively using PowerPoint*. Communication Skills Press.

Wempen, F. (2010). *PowerPoint 2010 bible*. New York: Wiley.

Conclusion

What we have learned in this book is how to conduct a very basic level of research in the field of economics. And even though this book specifically addresses the field of economics, it is perfectly clear that the concepts in it can be applied to any field where empirical work is used. As mentioned in the "Introduction," it may very well be the case that this book is too basic for those ivy-leaguers. Although I have seen many Ivy League PhD students who haven't a clue how to put together basic research. This tells me that many of their undergraduates wouldn't be able to either. Having said that, the target audience for this book is anyone that is interested in a brief, inexpensive guide on performing basic empirical research, putting it in writing, and presenting it to an audience.

The instructor will also notice that I leave plenty of room for elaboration. Indeed, in using this material in my own class, if I only presented this book, it would take about half of the semester; I enhance the topics in this book with exams on its subject matter, practice writing assignments prior to the final term paper, and further discussion within each area. This book is meant to supplement classroom instruction in a manner that is affordable to the student and helpful to the instructor. With that in mind, I hope you enjoyed it.

Note

Chapter 2

1. Mankiw, Romer, and Weil (1992); Islam (1995).
   Mankiw, Gregory, David Romer, and David Weil. 1992. *A Contribution to the Empirics of Economic Growth.* Quarterly Journal of Economics. Volume 107, Issue 2, pages 407–37.
   Islam, Nazrul. 1995. *Growth Empirics: A Panel Data Approach.* Quarterly Journal of Economics. Volume 110, Issue 4, pages 1127–70.

Index

A
Abstract of paper, 48, 49
Accounting paper, hypothesis, 40

B
Borders and shading options, 35

C
Coefficient distribution, 8
Coefficient estimates, 37
Cross-sectional analysis, 14

D
Data accuracy, 55–56
Data collection and formatting.
　See also Paper
　accuracy of, 55–56
　type of, 53–55
　usability of, 57–59
Data type, 13–14, 53–55
Data usability, 57–59
Dissemination, 47
Drafting and refining
　construction and contents, 65–67
　drafting process, 67–69
　fine tuning, 69
　paper formatting, 62–65
Drafting process, 67–69
Dummy variable construction, 24

E
EconLit's database, 46
Editing, equation, 31–33
Equation and variable
　description, 51
Equation editing, 31–33
Equation formatting, 13–14
Equation, screenshot of, 51
Estimation of equation, 2–12
Excel regression output, 4–5
Explanatory paper, hypothesis, 40

F
Fine tuning stage, 69
Fixed effects regression, 23–26
Formatting, equation, 13–14

G
Google, 45
Growth regressions, output for, 35

H
Hypothesis, 39–43

I
Inference, 2–12

L
Linear regression model, 10
Literature reviews
　gauge the work, 48–49
　performing the search, 47
　reading selected works, 49–53
　starting off, 45–47
Live audience
　addressing the, 72–73
　constructing slides, 71–72
　length of presentation, 73–76

M
Marginal effect, 6, 14
Microsoft PowerPoint, 72
Microsoft Word's equation
　editor, 31
Missouri Valley Economic
　Association, 73
Model calibration
　regression, 20–23
Model parsimony, 27–30
MS Word document, 32

N
Nonlinear function, 15

P

Panel data, 14
Paper
  abstract of, 48, 49
  accounting, hypothesis, 40
  drafting and refining, 61–69
  explanatory, hypothesis, 40
  formatting, 62–65
Parsimony, 27–30
p-values, 37

Q

Quadratic modeling and inference, 14–20
Quadratic regression, 18

R

Reading selected works, 49–52
Regression analysis and inference
  confident, 7
  data types, 13–14
  description, 1–2
  equation formatting, 13–14
  estimation and inference, 2–12
  excel regression output, for income, 4
  fixed effects regression, 23–26
  income vs. house prices, 3
  marginal effect, 6
  model calibration, 20–23
  model parsimony, 27–30
  quadratic modeling and inference, 14–20
  regression model, 1
  regression output for, 10
  Scatter plot of, 3
  slope and intercept, 3
  stata regression output, for income, 5
  stata's do-file, 4–5
  statistically significant coefficient, 8
  statistical significance, 6
  theoretical omitted variable bias, 20–23
  within transformation, 26–27
  using Excel, 3
  variables, 2
Regression model, 1
Research question, 39–43
Research topic choosing, 39–43
R-square value, 11

S

Scatter plot, 3
Slope coefficient, 8
Sophisticated research level, 14
Stata regression output, 5
Stata's do-file, 17
Statistically significant coefficient/relationship, 8
Statistical significance, 6

T

Table design, 33–38
Theoretical omitted variable bias, 20–23
Title page formatting, 64

V

Variable description, 51

W

Within transformation, 26–27

OTHER TITLES IN ECONOMICS COLLECTION

Philip Romero, The University of Oregon and Jeffrey Edwards,
North Carolina A&T State University, Editors

- *Managerial Economics: Concepts and Principles* by Donald Stengel
- *Your Macroeconomic Edge: Investing Strategies for the Post-Recession World* by Philip Romero
- *Working with Economic Indicators: Interpretation and Sources* by Donald Stengel
- *Innovative Pricing Strategies to Increase Profits* by Daniel Marburger
- *Regression for Economics* by Shahdad Naghshpour
- *Statistics for Economics:* Shahdad Naghshpour
- *How Strong Is Your Firm's Competitive Advantage?* By Daniel Marburger, Daniel
- *A Primer on Microeconomics:* Thomas Beveridge
- *Game Theory: Anticipating Reactions for Winning Actions:* Mark L. Burkey
- *A Primer on Macroeconomics:* Thomas Beveridge
- *Economic Decision Making Using Cost Data: A Guide for Managers* by Daniel M. Marburger
- *The Fundamentals of Money and Financial Systems* by Shahdad Naghshpour
- *International Economics: Understanding the Forces of Globalization for Managers* by Paul Torelli
- *The Economics of Crime* by Zagros Madjd-Sadjadi
- *Money and Banking: An Intermediate Market-Based Approach* by William D. Gerdes

Announcing the Business Expert Press Digital Library

*Concise E-books Business Students Need
for Classroom and Research*

This book can also be purchased in an e-book collection by your library as
- a one-time purchase,
- that is owned forever,
- allows for simultaneous readers,
- has no restrictions on printing, and
- can be downloaded as PDFs from within the library community.

Our digital library collections are a great solution to beat the rising cost of textbooks. e-books can be loaded into their course management systems or onto student's e-book readers.

The **Business Expert Press** digital libraries are very affordable, with no obligation to buy in future years. For more information, please visit www.businessexpertpress.com/librarians. To set up a trial in the United States, please contact **Adam Chesler** at *adam.chesler@businessexpertpress.com* for all other regions, contact **Nicole Lee** at *nicole.lee@igroupnet.com*.

www.ingramcontent.com/pod-product-compliance
Lightning Source LLC
Chambersburg PA
CBHW070601170426
43201CB00012B/1897